AGILITY

FOR STARTERS

FROM *ZERO* TO *HERO* IN *101* EXERCISES

Connie Sellers

with contributions from

Rosie Cavill • Greg Derrett • Denise Fenzi • Susan Garrett • Lee Gibson • Dave Munnings • Silvia Trkman

First published in 2016 by First Stone Publishing
St. Martin's Farm, Zeals, Warminster, BA12 6NZ, United Kingdom.

www.performancedog.co.uk

ISBN
978-1-910488-16-4
1-910488-16-X

Printed by Printworks Global Ltd., London & Hong Kong

Photography: Anne-Marie Waugh, Nick Ridley and Alan Castle.

Throughout this book the publishers use the pronoun 'he' in favour of 'he, she or it' but no
gender bias is intended in respect to either handler or dog.

KEY TO LINE DRAWINGS

H=handler

H A B C D =handler's position around course

A =assistant

T=training partner

D=dog

(Reward) =toy/treat

CONTENTS

INTRODUCTION

Agility is a fantastic sport, and your dog will love it as as much as you do. But even the best handlers needed a little help to get started.

Every dog must be taught basic skills and concepts before he attempts to run a course. This is called foundation training. I am passionate about developing a dog's desire to work with his handler, along with his drive to tackle an agility course.

Working as an agility instructor, and training my own dogs, I have devised a system of training that is based on creating value for what you want your dog to do. This may be powering ahead of you down a line of jumps, finding the correct weave entry or hitting the contact area on the agility equipment. But these elements of training have no intrinsic value for the dog; it is our job to give them value by rewarding them.

Clarity is the key, and in the 101 exercises outlined in this book, the emphasis is on rewarding the dog – with a toy or with food – at precisely the right moment so he is left in no doubt that you want him to take that line of jumps or wrap tightly around a jump wing. This enhances learning but, just as importantly, it builds trust between you and your dog which is essential for agility success.

Starting from from the earliest stages of training, the exercises will:

- Introduce your dog to agility equipment
- Encourage forward focus
- Teach handling techniques
- Resolve problems that may arise in training
- Establish a pattern of reward and reinforcement

Some of the exercises need no equipment, many of the others can be done with just a few

Connie Sellers: Agility instructor, Grade 7 handler, Crufts and Olympia finalist.

jumps or cones that will fit in your garden. There are some skills you can teach on your own, such as directionals, waits, wing wraps and weaves, but it helps enormously if you can work with a training partner when you are introducing your dog to new equipment, encouraging forward focus and teaching some of the handling moves.

I have learnt so much from teaching, and in the book I have included training tips that I have picked up from working with a wide variety of dogs and handlers. I have also been privileged to enlist the help of some of our top international handlers, and there are contributions from Susan Garrett, Dave Munnings, Lee Gibson, Denise Fenzi, Rosie Cavill, Silvia Trkman and Greg Derrett.

Taking part in agility means different things to different people. For some, the dream is to compete on the international stage, for others the goal is more modest – competing at a small show or attending group training sessions at an agility club. Whatever you decide to do, remember that agility is the greatest game you ever get to play with your dog, and your dog should think that, too.

I don't believe we win or lose – we simply keep on learning...

WHAT IS AGILITY?

It's fast and furious – and it is the most tremendous fun for dog and handler alike. It is a sport that is open to all, and if you work at training and motivating your dog, the sky's the limit. So what are the skills you will need?

The premise is simple: the dog that completes the obstacles, without faults, in the correct order, and in the fastest time, is the winner. But the sport has moved a long way from its debut in 1978 when it was staged as a demonstration at Crufts. Handling and training techniques have become increasingly sophisticated and a hundredth of a second can decide the top placings. The expertise required is addictive and it is now the fastest growing dog sport in the world with over 30 countries taking part in international competitions. So what is the secret of its success?

ANY DOG CAN DO IT

Agility is a sport for all, with classes divided into height categories so dogs of all sizes can compete. In most countries, including the UK and the USA, both pedigree breeds and mixed breeds can take part, so in this truly egalitarian sport a rescued mutt can compete on equal terms with his blue-blooded cousin. Border Collies and Working Sheepdogs dominate among the larger dogs and carry off the major prizes, but as long as your dog is fit and healthy, he can have a go. When you start off in agility, you and your dog will be in the lowest grade. As you become more experienced, the aim is to win out of the successive grades so you can compete at the top level.

ANY HANDLER CAN DO IT

At the top level, agility handlers need to be as fit as their dogs, with the ability to run and turn at speed. But this is a sport that encompasses male and female, young and old. As long as you have a good relationship with your dog, he will adapt to your handling style, regardless of whether it is lightning fast in a Championship final or a more sedate round at a fun show.

SIZING UP

In agility, dogs are measured and will use equipment which is appropriate to their size category. It is the height of the jumps, the height of the tyre and the length of the long jump that is affected. All the other equipment remains the same for all sizes.

Depending on the governing body, there are a number different size categories. Once you have had your dog measured, you can opt for the appropriate height.

AGILITY FOR STARTERS

Nothing beats the sheer joy of competing in agility – and that goes for both dog and handler. Pictured: Top international handler Silvia Trkman.

Photo: Monika Pleterski

Importantly, you do not need riches in order to train and compete. What you do need is time and commitment, so you get the very best from your dog.

WHAT MAKES AN AGILITY DOG?

All dogs are individuals and so there is no magic formula for the perfect agility competitor, but in general terms you are looking for:

- A dog with an athletic build that is kept at the correct weight for his size. This encompasses most types, but those with an exaggerated physique, such as the long-backed Dachshund or Basset Hound, or some of the giant breeds, should not be tested over agility equipment.
- Dogs cannot compete in agility until they are 18 months of age. However you can start training with agility equipment from 12 months. Foundation training, which does not involve equipment, e.g. forward focus (page 28) and teaching directionals (page 38), can start earlier.
- Agility is a sport, so your dog must have a reasonable level of fitness in order to take part.
- Dogs love agility and some get very excited. In a training group, dogs work in close proximity and need to be well socialised so they are not overawed by the situation.
- Your dog does not have to be an obedience champion, but you will need a basic level of control, which should include a solid response to verbal cues such as "sit" and "down", plus a reliable recall.

Does your dog meet these criteria? If so, agility could be the sport for you. Have a look at the exercises outlined in this book and see if you and your dog could make a winning combination. It will be fun to see what you and your dog can achieve but, remember, agility is a choice that you, not your dog, is making. You need to be 100 per cent sure that your dog is enjoying the challenge of training, and is always rewarded for working with you.

This is a sport where both you, and
your dog, need to be fit

BEFORE YOU START

Naturally you are keen to get started and have a go at all the agility equipment, but if you acquire some basic skills first you will have a far greater chance of being successful.

In agility, the dog works off-lead so he is free to do whatever he likes. You want him to run the course, following your directions – but what about that interesting smell that catches his attention halfway round? What about the dog in the training group who looks like such fun to play with? And if you get as far as competing at a show, will he make a beeline for the burger van?

In order to resist these temptations, your dog needs to view agility as the best fun in the world – and it is up to you to make him an eager convert. The key is motivation. Unless your dog has the drive to focus on what you are asking him to do, he will lose interest and become easily distracted.

There is no doubt that some dogs – and some breeds – are easier to motivate than others, but it is all about finding a reward that works for your dog, and then using it to reinforce the behaviour you want.

WHAT CONSTITUTES A REWARD?

Your dog is an individual and he will have his own ideas as to what he finds rewarding. You need to play with him and try out a few basic training exercises so you can observe his reaction to different types of reward. Work with a toy (there is a huge variety to choose from) and with food treats so you can see what excites him and what helps him to learn. Don't forget your role; you are giving the reward so, in your dog's eyes, you are golden. Back this up by giving verbal and/or physical praise so your dog sees you as the most fun person in the world.

One dog may be hugely motivated by a toy, another may be disinterested but then give the most perfect attention when you produce his favourite food treat. Or it could be that you need to mix it up a bit, using a combination of toys and treats depending on what you are trying to teach. Be flexible and, above all, listen to your dog; he will be giving you all the information you need.

To prevent injury when playing, your dog's head and neck should be in a straight line and he should be weight bearing on his hindquarters. Play should be back and forth – not side to side or up and down. If your training partner is rewarding, and the dog is running at full tilt, it may be necessary to drop the toy rather than risk whiplash, caused by the dog's head being jerked as he reaches for his toy.

THE REWARD THAT KEEPS ON GIVING

Toys and treats both have their part to play in agility training but I encourage all handlers to try to find a toy that their dog will work for as it can reward in so many different ways.

- As a handler you are involved in the game and your ability to make a toy 'come alive' will be highly valued by your dog. You provide the reward – and then you make it even better. No wonder he wants to work for you!
- A toy is highly visible and this is useful when you want your dog to focus ahead (see Forward Focus, page 28).
- You can vary the level of play and, therefore, your dog's level of arousal. Your dog will be quick to differentiate between a brief tug on his toy to encourage learning and an all-out game which means he has won the jackpot.
- You can swap toys depending on the exercise you are training and as a way of keeping your dog fresh and keen.

So even if your dog is reluctant to play at first, don't be too quick to give up and say he will only work for treats. If you put in some effort at this stage – finding a toy that your dog likes and showing him how to play – you will reap your own rewards later on.

FINDING A TOY

When you look at a stand full of dog toys, it is so easy to go for the one you like best – maybe its the colour or the design, or maybe its the type of toy that your previous dog loved. Well, you may strike lucky and find a toy that suits your dog, but it is so much better to do your homework and choose something he will view as a surefire reward.

Know your breed

Depending on your dog's genetic make up, there will be some toys that will be of intrinsic value to him because they strike a chord with instinctive behaviour that stems from his working ancestry. The gundog breeds with soft mouths, such as Labradors and Golden Retrievers love to retrieve, and they are likely to be motivated by a thrown toy they can run out and fetch. The herding breeds, such as Border Collies and Kelpies, want to chase, and so a toy that moves and 'comes alive' will be irresistible. In contrast, Terriers like to get hold of a toy and kill it, and so a tough, tuggy toy will work for them. The Toy breeds, such as Papillons and Chihuahuas, do not always have the best dentition and their preferred choice may be a toy that is small and soft, fitting easily into the mouth.

Know your dog

In most cases, a dog will conform to the inherited behaviour of his breed or breed type, but there is always the odd one out – the Collie that isn't interested in tugs and balls, the Labrador who would rather chase than retrieve, and the rescued mixed breed dog who gets worried the moment you produce a toy.

If the toy you are using is not rewarding, experiment and find something that does excite him. It could be that you need to make the game faster and more stimulating. Attaching a toy to a line and dragging it across the ground can work wonders. In the case of a worried dog, you may need to slow everything down so he doesn't feel over-faced. Or it may be that you need to observe your dog more closely to discover what he really likes. You may not regard a plastic bottle (without the top) or a knotted tea towel as the the best possible fun – but who cares what it is as long as your dog is engaged and happy!

Be sensitive to your dog's feelings and do not force him to play by thrusting the toy at him. This will have the reverse effect – your dog will back off and be even more reluctant to get involved. Make the toy exciting, moving it away from him, hiding it and then producing it from a different direction. He may be tentative at first but then he will start to show interest and, most importantly, it will be his decision and on his terms.

USING FOOD TREATS

Rewarding with food treats lacks the flexibility of toy-play, but it is a highly effective training tool. One of the biggest advantages of using treats is that you can vary the reward from high value to low value just by changing the food that is on offer. You can give dry kibble to reward an exercise your dog knows well but introduce something extra tasty, such as cooked liver, when you are teaching an exercise that is more challenging, or when you are training in a new place. Equally if a dog is becoming so food obsessed he can't think straight, you can downgrade your treats so he will focus on what you are asking him to do. A few points to bear in mind:

- Use small bite-size treats so your dog does not spend half an hour chewing his treat and 'forgets' what he is meant to be doing.
- Reduce your dog's daily food allowance depending on the number of treats you use. Remember, agility is for the lean and mean!
- There are times when you need to make the treat visible (a small piece of cheese will be easily obscured in grass) so you can use a treat pot, and balance one treat on the lid. You can also use a bait bag which serves the same purpose or, better still, a lotus ball with a treat secreted inside.

REWARD AND REINFORCEMENT

When you are training your dog, the reward – regardless of whether it is giving food or playing with a toy – should not be viewed as an end result. It is the means to an end; its effectiveness comes down to your skill as a trainer. It is your job to reward the behaviour you want, giving value to it, so your dog will repeat it. This is known as reward reinforcement, and if the reward is worth working for – and your dog understands what he has to do to get it – he will become a willing and creative partner.

It doesn't matter what the toy is as long as your dog likes it!

Greg Derrett says...

What is reward structure really about? It's being able to tell your dog he is brilliant while having fun. A key point to achieving great play is that you both enjoy it. Don't just play a token game of tug – really get into the game and be as enthusiastic as you can be. Are you both energetic, pulling hard against each other, both play-growling, while you are smiling and perhaps even laughing as you taunt him in a playful manner? Tease him with your free hand by slapping or grabbing at him, creating even more of a physical interaction. Remember, having that fun connection with your dog is what the whole game is all about, and believe me, that will leave a lasting impression on you both!

I was lucky enough to get into dog training as a kid, when I had less inhibitions about what I looked like and, if anything, people expected me to play with the dogs like an idiot! It is harder for an adult to lose those inhibitions and really play the game. But if you are both having so much fun that you actually forget what you look like, and you focus on rewarding your dog with the game – guess what? Now it truly is a reward!

Your goal should be to begin and finish every training session engaging in an energetic game with your dog, be it tug or,

Trainer's Tip

initially, just physical play. This routine will lead to creating a very strong association between:

PLAY = WORK = FOOD = WORK = PLAY
= HAPPY and ENTHUSIASTIC DOG!

TRILOGY OF LEARNING

When you are introducing your dog to agility, there are three stages of learning which can be applied in a variety of training situations.

This does not apply to contact equipment (the A-frame, dog-walk and seesaw), but it is useful when introducing the other pieces of equipment and when starting to combine obstacles. I suggest these stages of learning are taught without any equipment to begin with, only introducing equipment when your dog has fully understood what you want him to do.

In these exercises (and many of those that follow) you need a training partner who can restrain your dog or reward him depending what stage you have reached in your training. He or she is known as T in the line drawings. If your training partner is a fellow agility nut, you can swap roles so you both get a chance to handle your dogs.

EXERCISE 1

First step
The dog (D) is restrained by the training partner (T) holding him across the chest, by the collar or using a grab tag (a mini lead attached to the collar) which is best for dogs that are head shy or do not like being restrained by the collar. The handler (H) shows the dog he has a toy/treat and runs away, calling the dog and waving the toy/treat. While the handler is still running and the dog is raring to go, the training partner releases the dog, who sets off at full throttle to get his reward. The aim is to build up speed and motivation – agility training is the best fun in the world!

WHY WE LIKE RESTRAINING

If you pull a puppy towards you, he will pull away; if you try to push him down, he will push up. The puppy is not processing what he is doing, he is responding to a stimulus. This behaviour was first observed by Russian physiologist Ivan Pavlov in the 1890s, and he referred to it as the freedom reflex. It is now more commonly known as the opposition reflex and although it can create difficulties in training, such as when a dog pulls against you when he is on the lead, we can make real use of it in agility.

The key to agility training is to build motivation, increasing the dog's desire and commitment to take part. When the training partner restrains your dog, his instinct tells him to pull away. So, if he is focused on you – standing with his reward at the end of a line of jumps – everything is telling him to pull away and get to you as quickly as possible. Perfect!

The training partner needs to hold the dog firmly, but comfortably.

Timing is important in this exercise.

EXERCISE 2

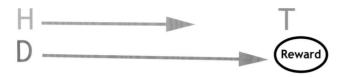

Second step

This time the roles are reversed. The handler (H) restrains the dog (D) and the training partner (T), armed with a toy/treat, runs away. The training partner needs to be irresistibly exciting, as this time you are asking the dog to leave the security of his handler. When the dog is straining forwards, fully focused on the training partner, the handler releases him and runs alongside – a mock up of running a course where the handler is often in this position. Some dogs find this difficult as they want to run to their handler. In this situation, the handler should hang back and the training partner puts in extra effort to lure the dog forwards – and the reward must be worth having.

EXERCISE 3

Third step

The first two steps of the trilogy – Exercises 1 and 2 – are relatively easy to achieve. This third step where the dog (D) is restrained by the handler (H) and must run to his reward without help from the training partner, should not be attempted until the first two stages are fully established. For this final stage of the trilogy you are asking your dog to work independently, running out to find his reward without outside help. If you are using food, you need to make it visible by placing a treat on the lid of your treat pot or by using a bait bag or a lotus ball. In this and subsequent exercises, I refer to a treat pot, but a bait bag or a lotus ball are equally effective.

As in all aspects of agility, you need to know your dog and progress at the pace that suits him. This applies every time you apply the trilogy of learning, regardless of the equipment or the exercise you are training.

Regardless of whether you are using food or a toy as a reward, you want your dog to get to it in record time...

GO TUNNEL!

The message you want to get over to your dog is that agility is fun, so I introduce the tunnel early on in training.

Most dogs find tunnels highly motivating, and because it is a relatively simple piece of equipment the success rate is high. Your dog will quickly build up speed, and you can be accurate with your timing when rewarding him.

There are two types of tunnel – a rigid, pipe tunnel which is open-ended, and a collapsible tunnel where the dog has to power his way through to open up the exit. For these early exercises, I use the rigid tunnel, which is easier to negotiate. Go to Exercises 47-50 to find out how to train the collapsible tunnel.

EXERCISE 4

For this exercise the tunnel is concertinaed to reduce the distance between the entrance and exit.

- Using step one of the trilogy, the training partner (T) restrains the dog at the entrance to the tunnel, making sure he is focusing on it, while the handler (H) goes to the tunnel exit with toy or treat. The handler establishes contact by calling the dog, and is ready to reward as soon as he emerges. There is minimal chance of failure as the dog is directed into the tunnel and then has the verbal encouragement of his handler to attract him. As soon as he knows a reward is at the end of the tunnel, he will start to build up speed. The training partner needs to hold the dog perfectly still – not thrusting him into the tunnel – as the dog needs to make the decision for himself.

THe tunnel is a natural draw for most dogs.

WHAT IF... Your dog is reluctant to go into the tunnel?

Although the tunnel is a relatively easy piece of equipment, some dogs are concerned about going into a dark space. This type of dog needs to know that the tunnel constitutes a direct route to his reward, and so he has nothing to fear. Whoever is at the end of the tunnel – training partner or handler – needs to establish contact, leaning into the tunnel and showing the toy/treat pot. This, coupled with lots of verbal encouragement, should do the trick!

EXERCISE 5

When your dog is powering through a concertinaed tunnel, you can increase the degree of difficulty by making it into a straight tunnel so your dog has to run the full length of it.

- Start with step one of the trilogy – training partner (T) restraining/handler (H) calling – to allow the dog (D) to get used to the longer tunnel.

EXERCISE 6

Once you dog is running the full length of the tunnel, training partner and handler swap roles.

- The handler (H) restrains the dog (D) at the mouth of the tunnel and and then runs alongside the tunnel as the dog runs through it.
- The training partner (T) is positioned at the tunnel exit to reward the dog – but the handler should step in and reward – giving another treat from the treat pot or continuing the game – as soon as possible.
- When it is clear that the dog understands the exercise, the handler can introduce a verbal cue, such as "tunnel" or "through".

WHY TRAIN ON BOTH SIDES?

In agility a dog is frequently required to swap sides and therefore he needs to be confident about approaching the equipment from either side, and take directions regardless of whether he is running on the handler's left or right side.

Dogs do not generalise, and just because your dog has learnt an exercise on the right side does not mean that he will automatically know what to do when you ask him to do it on the left side.

For this reason, all agility training involves working on both sides, in equal measure. This is particularly important when you are introducing new equipment or working on handling points.

- Try with the handler (H) running on the other side of the tunnel (below). By now the dog (D) understands the game and should be keen to get to the tunnel entrance as he knows his reward is with the training partner (T) at the other end.

- At this stage, the handler can step back a pace, allowing the dog to take the initiative and find the equipment.

EXERCISE 7

Now you can complete the trilogy of learning.

- The training partner is phased out so the dog (D) emerges from the tunnel to find his reward. The handler (H) should get to him as quickly as possible to give another treat or to instigate a game with the toy. This exercise can be practised with the handler running on both sides of the tunnel.

EXERCISE 8

Now the tunnel is curved which demands more commitment from the dog. Do not rush to get to this stage; you should have a number of sessions training with a straight tunnel before attempting it.

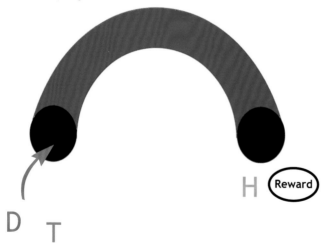

- Go back to step one of the trilogy with the training partner (T) restraining the dog (D) and the handler (H) recalling through the tunnel.

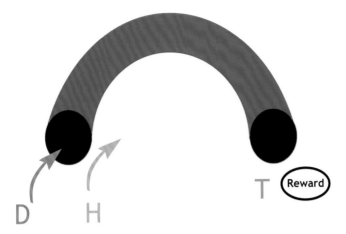

- You should be able to progress swiftly to step two of the trilogy, with handler (H) and training partner (T) swapping roles.

EXERCISE 9

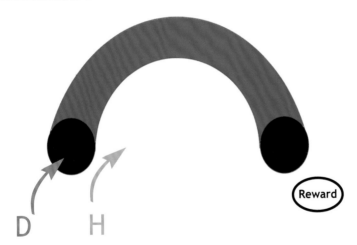

- The dog (D) is now working without direct encouragement from the training partner and so his training needs to be reinforced with successive repetitions and rewards. The handler (H) should swap sides, using the tunnel entrance on both the right and left-hand side, but always taking the shortest route, i.e. running on the inside of the tunnel.
- As the dog grows in confidence, the handler can release him from a greater distance and the treat pot/toy can be left further from the tunnel exit so he has to run a few paces before finding his reward.

FORWARD FOCUS

n agility, you want a dog that listens to you – but you also want him to use his initiative to a certain extent.

You don't want a dog that takes his own line and does any piece of equipment in whatever order he chooses, and neither do you want a dog that is glued to your side, constantly checking back to see if he doing what you want. The ideal agility dog is faster than his handler; you only have to watch your dog when he is free running to get an idea of his natural speed. He therefore needs forward focus so he can look ahead to see what obstacle he should tackle next, and then storm home to cross the finishing line ahead of you.

There are a number of exercises that will teach your dog to run ahead of you, all based on the certain knowledge that he is heading for a reward.

EXERCISE 10

For this you need a line of four jumps spaced 4m (13ft) apart (see page 29) – but, at this stage, you will not be using poles. You want your dog to be concentrating on running at speed through the wings; he does not need the added distraction of jumping.

- Do not be tempted to put poles on the ground between the wings thinking you are creating a more realistic set-up. A dog running at speed could easily trip over a pole and a broken toe could result.
- Introduce this exercise using step one of the trilogy of learning (training partner restraining the dog, handler calling).
- The training partner (T) is positioned at the start of a line of jumps (jump 1), restraining the dog (D); the handler (H) attracts the dog, calling him and showing a toy/treat pot, and runs between the wings (see line drawing top left, page 29).

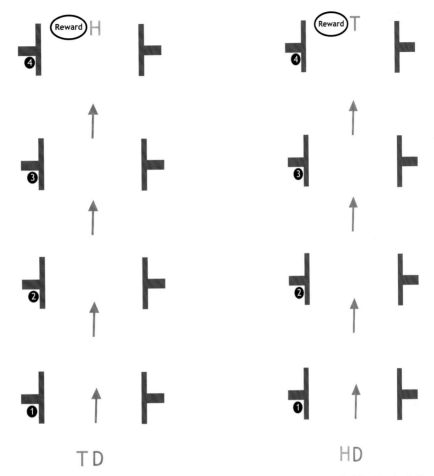

TD   HD

- Handler and training partner swap roles so the dog is now rewarded by the training partner (above right)
- Complete the trilogy of learning with the handler restraining the dog and then releasing him to run through the jump wings to find his reward without further assistance (page 30).

This is a fairly straightforward exercise but if your dog is struggling, make it easier by reducing the line of jumps to two, and then building up to four as he gains confidence.

Step three of the trilogy: The dog needs to have total confidence that he is running towards his reward.

EXERCISE 11

You will be using the same set-up as the previous exercise, but now you can introduce poles. These should be on the lowest level, regardless of the size of your dog. Initially, create a jump in the middle of the line (jump 2) as shown below, left.

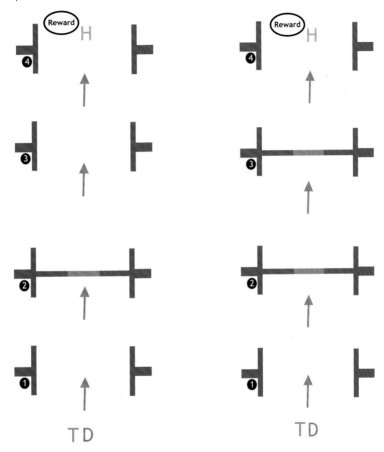

- Start off using step one of the trilogy of learning (training partner (T) restraining/handler (H) calling) so the dog (D) understands that although there is a jump in the equation, you are still asking the same thing from him.
- Add a pole to jump 3 (as shown above, right).

• Add a pole to jump 1.

• Add a pole to jump 4.

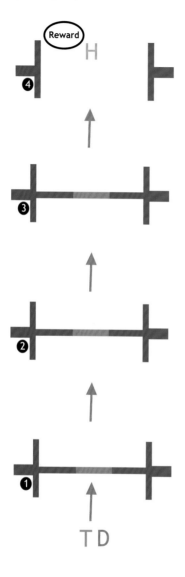

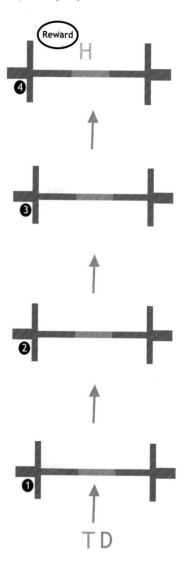

EXERCISE 12

If your dog is foot perfect in Exercise 11, you can quickly move on to step two of the trilogy where the handler and training partner swap roles.

- The handler (H) restrains the dog (D) and the training partner (T) attracts him with toy or treat. When the dog is fully committed to looking forward towards the training partner, the handler releases him and then runs alongside him (on the left-hand side), keeping to the outside of the jump wings.
- The handler can use a verbal cue, such as "go on" , encouraging the dog to take the jumps that lie ahead of him.

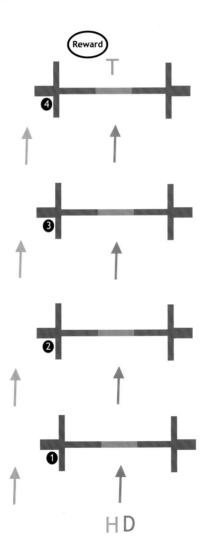

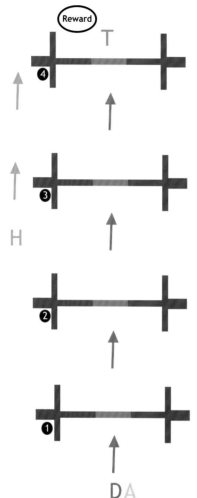

- To enhance learning, the handler (H) can move position and start halfway up the line of jumps. The training partner (T) needs to reward the dog after jump 4 so you will need to recruit an assistant (A) who can restrain the dog (D) in front of the first jump.

WHAT IF... Your dog veers off course and runs towards the handler rather than heading down the line of jumps?

- Make it easier by reducing the number of jumps.
- Try a few times with the hander stationary, so the dog focuses forward again and stops checking back to his handler.

Then ask yourself these questions:
- Is your reward good enough? If your dog does not value what you are offering, he will be easily distracted from the task in hand.
- Have you repeated this exercise too often?
- Is your dog is too tired to concentrate?
- Are you getting tired and losing your enthusiasm?

If your dog is struggling, do not repeat failures. Instead go back a stage. If you re-establish what you want and reinforce it with rewards, your dog will regain his confidence and, in no time, he will be ready for the next stage.

EXERCISE 13

Do not attempt this exercise until the previous exercise is well established. You want your dog to complete the exercise correctly but you do not want him to lose speed. You are are working with a line of four jumps, all with poles on the lowest level.

Pace progression so your dog does not lose speed or confidence.

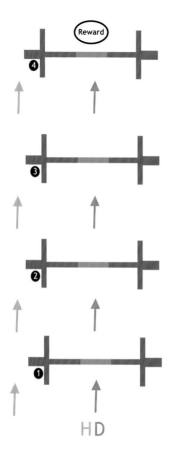

HD

- You are now ready to try step three of the trilogy of learning. The toy or treat pot is placed at the end of the line of the jumps and the training partner is out of the equation. It is essential that the dog sees the toy/treat pot being placed at the end of the line of jumps so he knows what he is aiming for. So first, the handler should take him to the toy/treat pot, and then run back with him to the start.
- The handler (H) restrains the dog (D) at the start of the line of jumps and waits until he is looking forward, focusing on the reward, before releasing him. The dog needs to be geed up with lots of verbal encouragement, so he is desperate to get to his reward.
- The handler releases the dog who takes the line of jumps. By this stage, he should be so focused on his reward that he pays no attention to the handler running alongside.
- If necessary the training partner can 'guard' the treat pot/toy, stepping aside when the dog is committed to jump 4.

WHEN DO THE JUMPS GO UP?

When dogs are doing their foundation training for agility, jumps are kept on the lowest height, regardless of whether your dog is small, medium or large. There is a lot to learn, so it is best if a dog can focus or what is being asked of him, following his handler's directions and maintaining his speed, without the distraction – and added pressure – of jumping at full height.

Once your dog has successfully completed the jumping exercises outlined in this book, start putting up the jumps. Initially, put up one or two jumps in a sequence so your dog adjusts to the new height. If your dog is large, progress from the lowest height to medium height before graduating to full size. Do not be in too much of a hurry to reach this stage otherwise you risk your dog going under jumps. A dog that progresses slowly will learn to sight the jumps; he will jump better, and he will understand that going under a jump is never an option.

Do not be in a hurry to put the jumps up to full height.

IN A SPIN

W hen you and your dog are working your way round an agility course, you need to give as much warning as possible of the direction you are taking. This is particularly important as your dog gains in confidence and is working ahead of you.

A dog who responds swiftly to "left" and "right" verbal cues will be able to maintain speed and accuracy as you are giving him the information he needs, not only to find the correct course, but also to adjust his body position accordingly. The simplest way to teach directionals is to train your dog to do left and right spins.

EXERCISE 14

It does not matter which directional you teach first – left or right – but it is important to opt for one and stick with it until the behaviour is fully established before moving on to the other one. For this exercise, I prefer to use treats to lure the dog into position. Once the behaviour is established, you can use a toy to speed him up.

- The dog should be standing facing the handler. To teach "left" the handler uses the hand holding the treat to 'draw' a full circle in an anti-clockwise direction.
- The treat should be held close to the dog's nose, and the circle should be drawn slowly to enable to the dog to follow the treat and be lured into turning a circle.
- When the dog is circling, albeit with the help of a treat, introduce the verbal cue, "left".
- After a number of repetitions, the handler uses an empty hand to draw the circle. He is ready to reward as soon as the dog has completed the circle with a treat, which he has been holding behind his back in the other hand.

WHAT IF... Your dog fails to follow the treat, which is being used as a lure?

- Make sure you have a high-value treat which your dog will find irresistible.
- Use your voice to encourage your dog and to make the exercise fun.

Initially use a treat to lure your dog. This dog is turning anti-clockwise, so the verbal cue is "left".

- If your dog is still struggling start off by luring him in a straight line so he gets the idea of following the treat.
- Sounds obvious, but your dog needs to be in a stand to start the exercise.

EXERCISE 15

The next stage is to wean the dog off hand signals. This should be done in stages. Remember to use the verbal cue "left" at every stage, so that there is a strong association between word and action.

- The handler draws three-quarters of a circle: when the dog completes the full circle, he gets his reward. The handler draws half a circle: when the dog completes the full circle, he is rewarded.
- The handler draws a quarter of a circle: when the dog completes the full circle, he is rewarded.
- The handler uses a flick of the wrist to indicate the direction – when the dog completes the full circle, he gets his reward.
- Now the handler can introduce the the verbal cue, "left" without the back up of a hand signal.

If you have taken your time working through the stages, your dog should have no problem understanding what you want. During the training process, reward for every spin.

EXERCISE 16

Now you are going to teach your dog a right-handed spin. Do not move on to this exercise until your dog has a 100 per cent success rate responding to his cue to go "left".

- Repeat Exercises 14 and 15 but this time the handler draws a clockwise circle. Initially you may need a treat to encourage the dog to turn.
- As the dog has already learnt to spin to the left, he will be quick to understand that he must now spin to the right. When the behaviour is clearly established you can introduce the verbal cue, "right" and fade out the hand signal.

DON'T BE A CON ARTIST!

When your dog does as you ask, reward him!
Sounds simple, but sometimes we humans take shortcuts and play
tricks on our dogs.
It usually happens when you haven't got a treat to hand, so what do you
do? You pretend...
  For example:

- Your dog has finished an exercise and you want him to come to you
  quickly so you can get back to the start. You get hold of his collar, and
  'lure' him to come with you, asking him to follow an invisible treat. He
  does as he asks because he trusts you – but you are cheating on him.
- You see his attention wander so you show him your closed fist, and
  ask: "What have I got?" The answer is nothing, but you have conned
  him into focusing on you and your non-existent treat.
- You ask your dog to do something, such as spin to the left. He does it
  beautifully, so you ask him to do it again, and again, and again. How
  does your dog view this? Without a tangible reward for a job well
  done, he will not only lose motivation, he will lose any perceived
  value in you and your rewards.

When you train your dog to work for a reward you are asking him to buy
into your game. Don't take advantage of him or he will quickly become
a non-believer.

NOW COMBINE IT

Your dog is now ready to combine two different pieces of equipment – the jumps and the tunnel. A small step forward, but you are beginning to get a feeling of what agility is all about.

EXERCISE 17

You will need to use a straight, rigid tunnel and place a couple of jumps at the end. The first jump should be positioned approximately 4m (13ft) from the tunnel exit, with the same gap between the first and second jump.

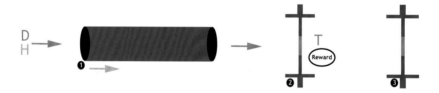

- With a confident dog, start this exercise on stage two of the trilogy with the handler (H) restraining the dog (D) at the mouth of the tunnel (obstacle 1), the training partner (with treat or toy) standing behind the first jump (obstacle 2).
- The dog, on the handler's left-hand side, needs to be focused on the tunnel. He is then released with the handler running along the right side of the tunnel.
- The training partner is ready to reward as the dog clears the jump.

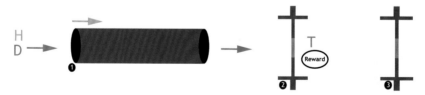

- Now try the exercise with the dog (D) starting on the handler 's right-hand side (H), and the handler running on the left side of the tunnel.

Your dog is now starting to look ahead for the the next obstacle on the course.

If your dog is unsure you can make the exercise easier by positioning the training partner at the tunnel exit. The dog can be rewarded here before adding in the jump.

EXERCISE 18

In this and subsequent exercises, there should be no need to work without poles unless a dog is lacking confidence with the jumps. However, poles should remain at the lowest height for all stages.

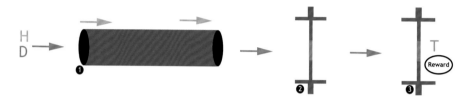

- Now the training partner (T) stands behind the second jump so the dog (D) has to combine three pieces of equipment – tunnel (1), jump (2), jump (3) – before getting his reward. Again, the handler (H) runs alongside the dog.

EXERCISE 19

When the dog is confidently firing through the tunnel with the handler running alongside on his right, it is time to swap sides.

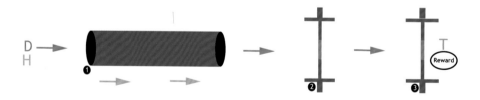

- Dog (D) and handler (H) start at the mouth of the tunnel but the dog is on the handler's left-hand side. The training partner (T) is in position behind the second jump, ready to reward.

EXERCISE 20

Up until now, the training partner has been playing an active part, attracting the dog and offering the reward. In time you will want to increase the difficulty to stage three of the trilogy where the training partner is no longer part of the exercise. This means the dog has to work independently, trusting that he will find his reward when he has completed the exercise. It is a big ask, so take your time and make sure your dog fully understands the exercise and is motivated to fire on all cylinders in the certainty that his toy/treat is ready and waiting!

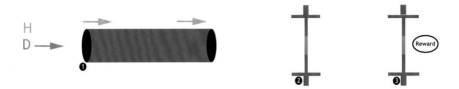

- Dog (D) and handler (H) start at the tunnel entrance, and the handler runs alongside after releasing the dog. It is advisable to ask the training partner to 'guard' the toy or treat pot, stepping aside when the dog is committed to the second jump.

EXERCISE 21

To improve tunnel drive, extend the distance to the tunnel entrance. For this, and the following three exercises, you will need four cones, placed half a metre (18 inches) apart in line with the mouth of the tunnel.

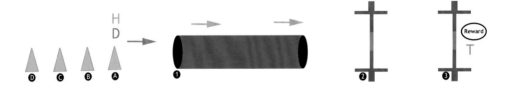

- Dog (D) and handler (H) stand level with cone A. The dog is then released to go through the tunnel and over the jumps to reach the training partner (T) and reward.

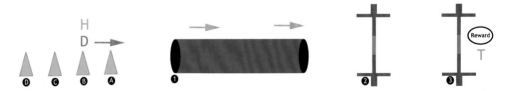

- Dog (D) and handler (H) start from cone B.

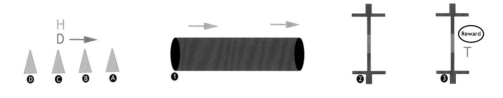

- Dog (D) and handler (H) start from cone C.

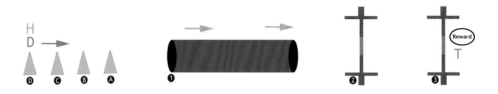

- Dog (D) and handler (H) start from cone D. Now the dog has a to cover a good distance to reach the tunnel, which – with the added stimulation of being restrained – will encourage him to run at full speed.
- Complete the trilogy, withdrawing the training partner from the exercise.
- Now repeat on the other side.

EXERCISE 22

Dog and handler are ready to reverse directions which means the dog has to clear the jumps before finding the tunnel. The dog has started his combination training by focusing on the tunnel – which is a natural draw – and now he has to negotiate the jumps before reaching the tunnel, which increases the degree of difficulty.

- To make things easier, dog (D) and handler (H) start on jump 2. The training partner (T) – with treat or toy – is ready to reward at the tunnel exit.
- When the dog is looking forwards, he is released to clear the jump and then he must find the tunnel entrance.
- The training partner rewards the dog as he emerges from the tunnel.

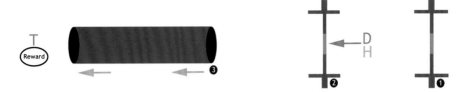

- Try the exercise with the dog (D) starting on the handler's right side in front of jump 2.
- The dog takes the jump and heads for the tunnel, with the handler running along the left side of the tunnel.
- The training partner (T) is in position at the tunnel exit, ready to reward.

EXERCISE 23

Again, the training partner (T) stays in position at the tunnel exit, ready to reward.

- Dog (D) and handler (H) start behind jump 1 so the dog has to negotiate three obstacles, with the handler running alongside, before he is rewarded by the training partner. After a few repetitions, the handler (H) can swap sides and run on the left side of the dog (D).

WHAT IF... Your dog clears the first jump and then heads for his reward?

The training partner needs to establish contact with the dog through the tunnel by crouching down and calling him.

EXERCISE 24

When you think your dog is ready, you can apply stage three of the trilogy where the training partner is taken out of the equation. The dog must now work independently, with the handler running alongside, aiming for his reward which is positioned at the tunnel exit.

EXERCISE 25

You will be using the same set basic set up – a rigid tunnel and two jumps – but this time the tunnel is curved. Position the jumps on the right side.

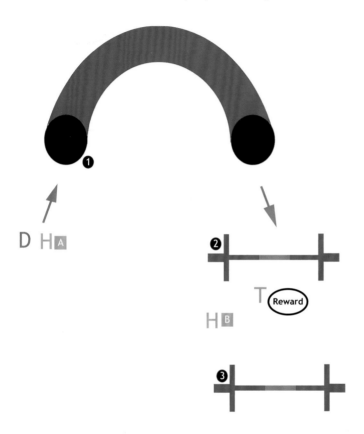

- Dog (D) and handler HA) start at the mouth of the tunnel; the dog is on the handler's left-hand side. The training partner (T) – with treat/toy – stands behind the first jump.
- When the dog is focused on the tunnel entrance, he is released and must exit the tunnel and clear the first jump before getting his reward. The handler runs alongside on the inside of the the tunnel, which is the shortest route, to HB.

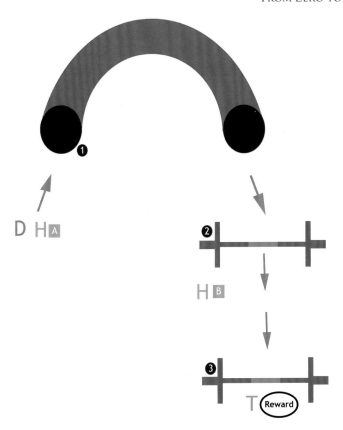

D H_A

H_B

T (Reward)

- Now the training partner (T) stands behind the second jump so the dog (D) has to go through the curved tunnel and over two jumps. The handler (H_A) starts alongside the dog at the mouth of the tunnel and is ready at position H_B to guide him, with left arm, over the two jumps as he emerges from the tunnel.

What If? ...Your dog will not focus on the tunnel ahead and keeps looking back at the reward?

- The training partner, with toy or treat, should stand further back or keep out of the way until the dog is committed to the tunnel.
- For a couple of repetitions, the handler can also use a toy or treat to get the dog fully focused before he sets off.

EXERCISE 26

You need a curved tunnel and two jumps, but this time the jumps are positioned on the left.

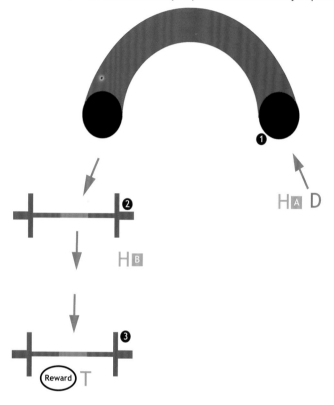

- Repeat Exercise 25 with the dog negotiating the tunnel (1), jump (2), jump (3), but this time the dog is positioned on the right-hand side of the handler (H$_A$). Again the handler (H$_B$) takes the shortest route; the training partner (T) is ready to reward after the second jump.
- When you are confident that your dog understands the combination of a curved tunnel and two jumps, you can move on to stage three of the trilogy and take the training partner out of the equation so the dog runs to a dead toy or to his treat pot, with handler running alongside. Do not be in a hurry to do this – you want to keep your success rate high.

EXERCISE 27

For this exercise you need a curved tunnel and four jumps, positioned 4m (13ft) apart.

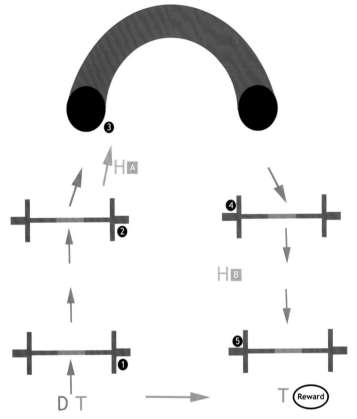

- The training partner (T) restrains the dog (D) behind jump 1. The handler (HA) is positioned between jump 2 and the tunnel entrance with his left arm (nearest the tunnel) outstretched.
- As soon as the dog is released the handler points to the tunnel. Once the dog is committed to the tunnel, the handler moves to position HB and uses his left arm to show which route to take.
- As soon as the dog is committed to the jumps, the training partner moves over to stand behind jump 5, ready to reward.

WHAT IF... Your dog runs round the jumps and makes straight for the tunnel?

- The handler needs to establish a connection with the dog through the wings by making eye contact and ensuring the left arm is clearly indicating the route to take.
- If the dog is still struggling, take out the poles to make the exercise easier. You should replace them as soon as the dog understands what you want.
- If the dog is still missing out the jumps, the handler can reward after jump 2, until the behaviour is fully established.

EXERCISE 28

When your dog is ready, apply stage three of the trilogy with the dog (D) running to a dead toy or treat, with handler (H) running alongside. In this exercise, the training partner (T) will still be involved, restraining the dog at the start. You are asking your dog to negotiate five pieces of equipment without help, so play it safe and delay this stage until you are sure your dog is ready to cope.

Your dog understands the notion of running to a dead toy, learnt at the beginning of his foundation training.

CONTROLLING THE REWARD

There are times when you want your dog to be thinking about what lies ahead on the course, which is why you train him to focus ahead, driving towards his reward. But what happens when your dog makes a mistake, yet gets to his toy or treat pot and self-rewards? In this instance, the dog has learnt absolutely nothing – apart from the fact that he can get his reward any time he likes. It is therefore essential to build in an element of control.

You need your training partner to 'guard' the toy or treat pot. Now send your dog, but before he reaches his reward, call him to you and instantly reward him with another toy or a high value treat. If he fails to come to you, your training partner will ensure that he cannot get his toy or treat, so he will realise that he has to try again to get his reward. When your dog starts to get the idea, you can use a verbal cue – I use "woopsie" – which will call him away from the reward ahead of him.

When you are practising this, you need to send your dog direct to his reward at least 50 per cent of the time otherwise he will lose his forward focus.

What if... Your dog keeps running forwards to his reward, even though it is guarded?

Make sure the toy/treat you have is of greater value than the reward on offer at the end of the exercise.

What if... Your dog values one of his toys above the other and seeks out his 'favourite'?

In this case, you need to offer two identical toys.

See: Keep It Positive, page 105.

FAN-TASTIC

U p until now, your dog has been jumping in straight lines; he now needs to learn how to turn. The best way of doing this is to set up a fan of jumps, where he has to be more aware of the handler's driving arm (see page 56), showing him where to go. He will also be learning how to check his stride and turn.

EXERCISE 29

For this exercise you need three jumps, positioned 2m (6.5 ft) apart, set in the shape of a fan. By this stage, your dog should be happy jumping with the poles on the lowest height so, even though this is a new exercise, there is no need to backtrack to using jumps without poles.

- Start with stage two of the trilogy with the handler (Hᴀ) restraining the dog (D) in front of jump 2 of the fan.

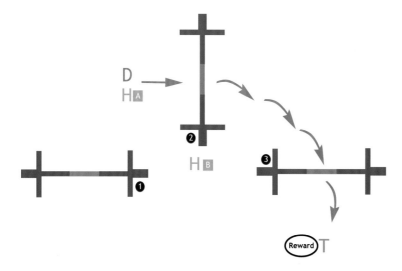

- The handler (HA) releases the dog and then moves to the outside of the wing (position HB) and uses his driving arm (nearest the dog – in this case the left arm) to go over jumps 2 and 3.
- The training partner (T) is in position behind jump 3, ready to reward, but is careful not to lure the dog. The dog needs to think for himself and complete the exercise in order to get his reward.

What if ....your dog is trying to follow you rather than taking the jumps?

- Remove the poles and work with your dog running through the wings until he understands what is required. Then try again with poles in place.

EXERCISE 30

This is a repeat of Exercise 29 but now incorporating all three jumps.

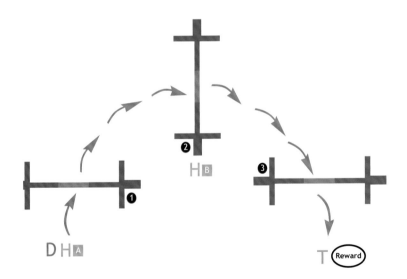

- This time the dog (D) and handler (HA) start in front of jump 1.
- The handler (HB) takes the shortest route on the inside of the jump wings, guiding the dog with his driving arm (nearest the dog – in this case the left arm), so that he goes over all three jumps of the fan before getting to the training partner (T) and his reward.
- At this stage the handler can use the verbal cue. "right".

IN THE DRIVING SEAT

When handling a dog in agility, you can establish greater clarity if you use a 'driving' arm to show the dog which obstacle he should take and which direction you are moving in.

The golden rule is that your driving arm is always the one nearest the dog – so when your dog is on your right use your right arm; when he is on your left, use your left arm.

The driving arm clearly indicates where the dog should be going.

WHAT IF... Your dog is too fixated on the training partner (and the reward) and goes around the jumps?

- The training partner should try standing further back.
- For a couple of repetitions only the handler should have a toy/treat so the dog re-focuses.
- An assistant restrains the dog, allowing the handler to stand between jumps 1 and 2 which clarifies the route the dog needs to take.

EXERCISE 31

When the dog can do a fan of jumps, working on the handler's left hand-side, it is time to teach him to do it on the right.

- The handler (HA) and dog (D) should start in front of jump 2. The handler moves around the inside of the fan to position HB using his right arm as his driving arm. The training partner is positioned behind jump 3 ready to reward the dog.

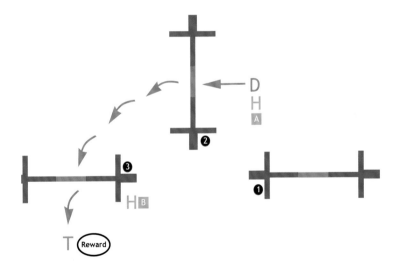

EXERCISE 32

Now the dog (D) and handler (Hᴀ) start in front of jump 1. The handler releases the dog, moving to position Hв. The dog completes all three jumps to reach the training partner (T) and his reward. The verbal cue is "left".

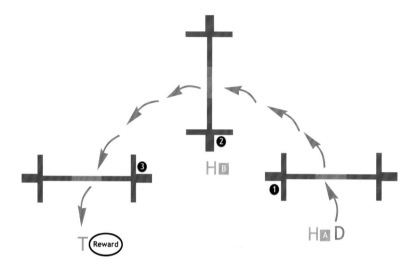

When the time is ripe, take the training partner out of the equation so the dog (D) sets off with the handler (Hᴀ) who moves around the inside of the jumps to Hв, using his driving arm to guide the dog over all three jumps. His reward is positioned after jump 3.

CAUGHT ON CAMERA

Now you are starting to handle your dog, ask your training partner to film what is going on. In agility everything happens at such a fast pace, you cannot be certain that your timing and body language is correct (see Picking up clues, page 138). You also need to check that you are using the correct driving arm.

Study the live footage so you can see if your cues and signalling make sense to the dog and then you can fine tune accordingly.

FROM ZERO TO HERO IN 101 EXERCISES

*Your dog is now
negotiating a fan of jumps
and is learning how to
follow the driving arm.*

WAIT FOR IT

A t the outset of an agility round, you do not want to start level with your dog. You will give yourself a huge advantage if you can get ahead and then recall him.

You have probably taught your dog to "wait" for pet obedience; but for agility you need to ensure he is 100 per cent reliable – even when he is on the start-line at a show. It does not matter what position your dog adopts – 'sit', 'stand' or 'down' – when he is asked to "wait". It is a matter of which position he finds most comfortable. If he feels secure, he is less likely to break position.

EXERCISE 33

Experiment by luring your dog into a 'sit,' a 'stand' and a 'down', and assess which position comes most naturally to him. If your dog is excitable, you may well find a 'down' is the best option. Once you have decided on your dog's 'wait' position, you must be entirely consistent and make sure you always leave him in that position.

- Now ask him to "wait". Leave him a few paces and then return to him and reward. In this instance, reward with treats rather than a toy as you want him to stay calm. You can build in a toy as your training progresses.
- Build up the distance you can leave him, and the duration of the 'wait'.
- Leave him from the left side and from the right side.
- Change directions, walking in front of him, to the side and behind him so that he learns to "wait" regardless of your position.
- Make it harder by jogging away from your dog and moving your arm up and down. Try stopping, starting and stopping again before going back to reward. Keep testing, so your dog learns that he must "wait" until he is released, regardless of what you are doing.

EXERCISE 34

Now work on recalling your dog from the 'wait', just as you would at the start of an agility course.
- Place a toy/treat pot (with a treat on the lid) at a short distance, in line with your dog.
- Give your dog his verbal cue, "wait" and leave him a short distance. You can do this without equipment, or you can position yourself by a jump wing to make it more realistic.
- As you walk away, use your driving arm to show the line you want your dog to take.

You need to teach your dog self-control which is not easy if he is highly motivated...

- Halt midway between your dog and where you have placed his reward. Release him with a verbal cue, such as "OK", and he will head straight for his toy/treat pot. This teaches him that he must wait to be released, and also to focus ahead rather than coming to you.

EXERCISE 35

Throughout your training, you need to build up value for the 'wait' position so that it is golden. Ask your training partner to 'guard' the toy while you are teaching this exercise.

- If you dog breaks, go back and put him back in his correct 'wait' position. Do not reprimand him or give verbal encouragement. Simply put him back in position and walk away. Your dog needs to learn that he will only be rewarded for maintaining his 'wait' until he is released – no matter how many times you have to put him back in position. If he keeps failing, try leaving him a shorter distance.
- Get into the habit of rewarding the 'wait' on a random basis whenever you are training. Your dog may know the lesson by heart, but if his behaviour is continually reinforced – especially in new places – he will be even more reliable. Remember, success rate needs to be high at every stage before you increase the degree of difficulty.

WHAT IF... Your dog has a perfect wait at home, but he breaks position with the added excitement of working in a group, or when he is put in front of agility equipment?

- Create value for what you want, rewarding the 'wait' with a high-quality treat or a game with his favourite toy.
- If your dog breaks his 'wait', return to him, and put him back in position.
- Practise your 'wait' in lots of different places, adding distractions such as people and other dogs, as he becomes more reliable.

EXERCISE 36

You can now work on a routine which you can use at the start of every course. The aim is to get your dog focused on you regardless of what is going on around him. This is useful in a group training situation and essential if you are getting ready on the start-line in a competition. It is all too easy for adrenaline to take over, so a highly motivated dog needs a start-line routine to calm him and get him into a working frame of mind. A set routine is equally, if not more, important for an anxious dog as it helps him to concentrate on the job in hand rather than worrying about what is going on around him. From the moment you unclip the lead, you want your dog to be connected to you, waiting for his instructions.

A start-line routine can take a number of different forms with the dog:

- Walking to heel and then going into the start position ('sit', 'stand' or 'down').
- Doing an obedience finish, starting in front of the handler and then going behind their legs to adopt the start position on the handler's left or right-hand side.
- Facing the handler, doing a half circle behind the handler, emerging in the gap between the handler's legs and going into a 'sit' or a 'down'.
- Doing leg weaves for a few paces, and then going into the start position.

It doesn't matter what you do – just something that comes easily to your dog – and then you can reward him before giving his cue to "wait". When your dog has learnt his start-line routine, you can give a verbal cue such as "Get ready!"

THE GREAT LEAP FORWARD

When your dog has a reliable 'wait' and responds to his release command "OK", you can make huge progress in your agility training as now you can work on exercises without needing to restrain your dog. He is learning to work independently and as you create distance from him he will become practised at reading your body language and responding to your signals. Now you can try all the exercises outlined so far, but this time leaving your dog in the 'wait' and then recalling him from a distance.

Do not be too ambitious to start with; it is better that your dog learns to wait and is constantly rewarded for it rather than pushing him too far. A dog will be quick to learn bad habits – breaking position or creeping forward – and it will take you a long time, and a lot of hard work, to resolve the problem.

Although you can now use the 'wait' in training, there will be times when a restrained start is still useful, particularly if your dog is losing motivation and needs geeing up.

Dave Munnings says...

Every dog is different; work with the dog you have. They all have their own strengths and weaknesses the same as we do, so our job is to figure out how to use those to our advantage and get the best out of them. Finding that "switch" that makes them want to try their hardest isn't always easy, but every dog has it, it's just a case of looking hard enough.

Not every dog is capable of being a world champion, but using mainly positive reinforcement training and NO positive punishment will help every dog to fulfil his potential. Sometimes it's the partnership that works. Our dogs should be our best friends; the better relationship you have with your dog, the harder he will try for you and the more fun you will both have. So before you start any agility training, get the relationship right.

Be CONSISTENT with your training and remember that agility is a game for them; they don't know if they win or lose. Have fun with your dogs, enjoy training them and never blame them for the mistakes we make in our training and handling. Our job is to make them think everything is fun. If they don't like to wait on the start line or stop on their contacts, it's because you have made those places boring. Everything should be a game; if they enjoy something and value it then they will do it again.

If you are inconsistent this will produce grey areas in your training, and as soon as you get the grey areas then your dogs will be confused. This will lead to frustration and possible displacement

Trainer's Tip

behaviours. Before you try to 'fix' these issues, look at yourself and ask "What am I doing wrong that is causing this?", then fix that first.

My main tip is have fun. Don't take it too seriously. Our dogs are never with us long enough, so make the most of the precious time you have with them.

Yulia Titovets

ADDING TO IT

> **N**ow your dog is used to combining different pieces of equipment (jumps and tunnel) and has learned to jump a fan of jumps, you can put them together. He needs to listen to you and follow your driving arm in order to take the right course.

EXERCISE 37

For this exercise you will need five jumps and a rigid tunnel which needs to be curved.

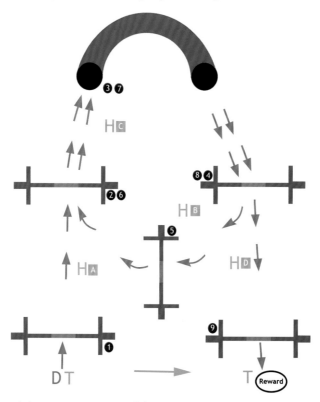

- The dog (D) and training partner (T) are positioned behind jump 1 and the handler (HA) leaves from the left-hand side to stand between jumps 1 and 2 with driving arm outstretched.
- The dog is released and as he takes the first jump, the handler moves off to show him the second jump and then gives the "tunnel" command.

- As the dog emerges from the tunnel, the handler (HB) picks him up and takes him round the fan of jumps (jumps 4, 5 and 6) using the verbal cue "right" . The handler turns his shoulders to the right which will tell the dog which way to go.
- When the dog is committed to jump 6, the training partner can move to stand behind jump 9, ready to reward.
- As the dog clears jump 6, the handler (Hc) directs him to go into the tunnel (7) for a second time.
- As the dog emerges from the tunnel, the handler (HD) picks him up and encourages him to go down the line of jumps (jumps 8 and 9) with a "go on".
- The training partner can encourage the dog by calling him and is ready to reward when the exercise is completed but the handler should take over immediately, so the dog is being rewarded by the person he has worked for.

EXERCISE 38

When your dog has mastered Exercise 37, you can swap sides so he has to go round the fan of jumps from the left.

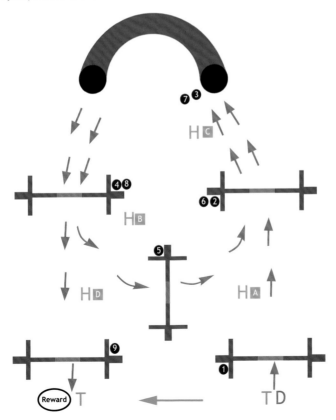

WHAT IF... Your dog fails to take jump 2 and heads straight for the tunnel?

- To clarify the line you want your dog to take, the handler can move and be positioned beyond the second jump. You can also reward your dog at this point before heading for the tunnel.

EXERCISE 39

You are asking a lot in the previous two exercises so do not be in too much of a hurry to move on to step three of the trilogy, taking the training partner out of the equation. However, it is an important stage to master as your dog is becoming increasingly aware of the fact that you give the directions and you provide the reward. Obviously your dog needs to have a reliable "wait" before attempting this exercise.

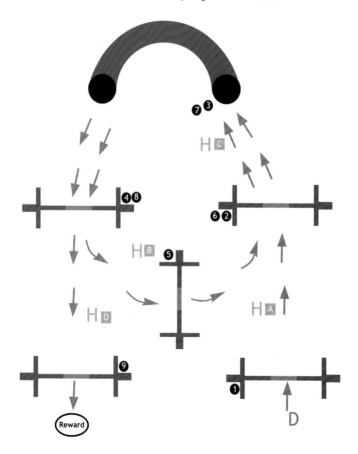

You and your dog are now beginning to work as a partnership.

WHAT IF... Your dog goes wrong on the course?

- Remember you are training and your dog is learning – errors are inevitable. You need to correct a mistake but you don't want your dog to feel flattened or confused.
- The best plan is to repeat the obstacle where your dog has gone wrong as quickly as possible and then complete the course so your dog can get to his reward without further delay.
- Do not go back to the start of the course. It may seem logical to you to get the whole thing right but your dog will not understand where he went wrong, why you are going back to the start, or why he is having to work for longer without getting a reward.

Remember, it is your responsibility to get your dog to his reward as quickly as possible.

TRAINING SANDWICH

When you are structuring a training session, think in terms of a meat-filled sandwich:

Top layer: Start with something achievable – and enjoyable! You want to make a confident start to the training session so your dog is raring to go.

Filling: Go for something meaty, such as introducing a new exercise, or completing the final stages of work in progress.

Bottom layer: End with something easy. You and your dog will both be tiring so don't fall into the trap of starting something that is too hard to finish. You want your dog to finish before he is ready, to maintain his keenness and enthusiasm.

GO LONG

This obstacle requires the dog to stretch out as he jumps rather than going up and over, which he has learnt to do over upright jumps. This piece of equipment causes few problems, but it is important that dogs respond to a verbal cue so they can change their stride and cover the distance.

EXERCISE 40

The long jump is set up with a marker pole on all four corners to guide the dog. When you are introducing the long jump, use these even when it is not at its full extent as it will help to keep your dog on the correct line.

- If you have a small dog, use one plank of the long jump; medium and large dogs can start with two planks.
- Begin with step one of the trilogy with the training partner (T) restraining the dog (D) at the start of the jump, with the handler (H) in position to reward at the end of the jump.
- For small dogs, increase to two planks; three planks for medium and large dogs.

To prepare your dog for the long jump, you will need to use a different verbal cue from the one you use for upright jumps.

- Now add a third plank for small dogs. This is the full extent of the long jump for this size category.

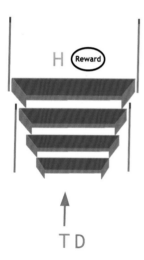

- For medium and large dogs, add a fourth plank with training partner restraining and handler rewarding.

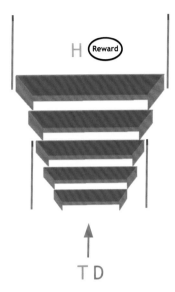

- Large dogs will need a fifth plank added.

Remember, the long jump is built as an ascending ladder with the lowest plank at the start and the highest plank at the end. You need to use this pattern, regardless of how many planks your dog is jumping.

EXERCISE 41

Now move on to step two of the trilogy with the training partner and handler (H) reversing positions. Keep the long jump at the specified length for small, medium and large dogs.

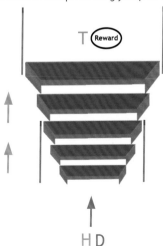

- At this stage, introduce a verbal cue, such as "long" so the dog has advance warning that he must change pace in order to clear the long jump.

EXERCISE 42

Complete the trilogy with the handler (H) releasing the dog (D) to find his reward without the training partner's help. The handler runs alongside.

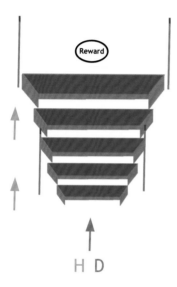

- Now repeat the exercise with the handler running on the other side.
- When your dog is tackling the long jump with confidence, add a jump before and after the obstacle so he learns to negotiate it within a course.

WHAT IF... Your dog banks the long jump or scrabbles over it?

- Most dogs learn to adjust their strides after a few attempts and clear the long jump with ease. But if your dog is struggling, reduce the number of planks and only add to them when your dog is jumping cleanly.
- Put jump wings on either side so it looks more like a conventional jump.
- Increase the run up so your dog has more speed and power when he takes off. This is particularly helpful for small dogs.

VERBAL CUES

It is a human characteristic to give a name to everything we see and do, and the sooner we do it the better, so we can communicate with our fellow humans. However, a dog's brain works in a completely different way, as words in themselves have no meaning. A dog learns by association, and so he will learn that the verbal cue "long", for example, means go to that piece of equipment, simply by repetition; he associates the word with the action. By reinforcement – rewarding him for the 'correct' response – he will produce the desired behaviour on cue. For this reason, in most training scenarios, verbal cues are not introduced until the dog fully understands the exercise.

You can choose your own verbal cues to label the equipment or behaviour you require, but bear in mind:

- Keep verbal cues short and simple – for the dog's sake and because you will run out of steam if you have too much to shout out as you run round an agility course.
- You must be consistent and always use the same word for the piece of equipment or behaviour you have labelled.
- Speak clearly and be aware of your tone of voice. In your desire to communicate, it is all too easy to start barking commands, which may be off-putting for a more sensitive dog.
- Don't use words that are part of your everyday repertoire. It will be highly confusing for your dog and could have a negative effect if you are using words such as 'no' or 'leave' when you are trying to prevent your dog self-rewarding.

In addition to naming the equipment, you will need verbal cues to:

- Tell your dog to "wait" on the start line
- Release from the start line or from a contact (e.g. "OK")
- Stop in position on a contact (e.g. "touch"). *See Touch it, page 96.*
- Tell him to go "left" or "right", identify handling moves, e.g. "wrap", and take the line of equipment that lies ahead, "go on".

Lee Gibson says...

www.firstcontactagility.co.uk

Trainer's Tip

www.firstcontactagility.co.uk

When handling your dog, you need to consider both the path of the dog around the course, and your own path (as the handler). They are not the same.

Many handlers feel they are getting too close to their dog's lines, so that they have to run 'around' equipment instead of moving in a straight line, supporting the dog on the line he is set on.

Remember that body language needs to reinforce what you are saying, not contradict it. This is especially true in obstacles such as the long jump, when the handler needs to set his line, and the dog's line, relatively early to achieve maximum efficiency!

Photo: Clair Humphreys.

TYRE PRACTICE

The tyre can be introduced at any stage in your training programme, although your dog may find it easier if he is already jumping confidently. This is not a difficult piece of equipment; it is more a matter of the dog learning to sight it.

EXERCISE 43

The tyre can be positioned at three heights depending on whether your dog is small, medium or large. Initially, start with the tyre on the height for small dogs, even if your dog is medium or large.

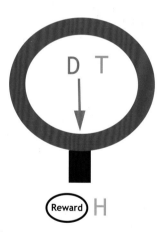

- Start with step one of the trilogy with the training partner (T) and dog (D) positioned in front of the tyre and the handler on the other side with the reward. For this piece of equipment the handler can lure the dog by putting his arm, with treat or toy, through the tyre.
- The training partner releases the dog, which is called by the handler through the tyre and rewarded.

A verbal cue, given in advance, will help your dog to sight the tyre.

EXERCISE 44

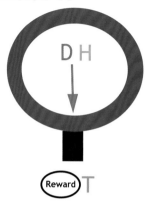

- Swap roles so the hander (H) restrains the dog (D) and the training partner (T) calls him through. After releasing the dog, the handler runs alongside the tyre.
- When your dog clearly understands what is required, the handler can introduce a verbal cue, e.g. "tyre".
- The training partner can stand further and further back so the dog has to make the decision to jump through the tyre, rather than being lured.

EXERCISE 45

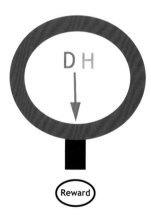

- When your dog is confident with Exercise 44, move on to the third step of the trilogy with the dog going through the tyre to find his reward, without the help of the training partner.
- Repeat the exercise with the handler running on the other side.

EXERCISE 46

If you have a medium dog, you can now try with the tyre at the correct height for this size category. If you have a large dog, try a few repetitions at medium height before attempting full height. Do not attempt this until your dog is happy jumping through the tyre at its lowest level. Unless your dog is struggling with this piece of equipment, there is no need to repeat steps one and two of the trilogy when the height of the tyre changes – you can proceed straight to step three.

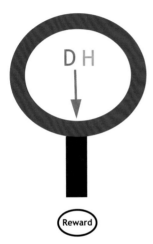

- When your dog is tackling the tyre at full height, add a jump before and after the obstacle so he learns to negotiate it within a course.

WHAT IF... Your dog keeps running past the tyre to get his reward?

Go back to step one of the trilogy (training partner restraining, handler on the other side of the tyre) so the handler can lean through the tyre showing the treat or toy. This makes it very obvious for the dog and will give him added motivation if he feels a little unsure.

POWERING THROUGH

As far as you are concerned, a tunnel is a tunnel, regardless of whether it is a rigid, pipe tunnel or a flat, collapsible tunnel, which the dog has to push through to find the exit. However, a dog's mind does not work in the same way, and even though he is happy to go through a rigid tunnel, he will regard the collapsible version as a completely different piece of equipment.

The collapsible has an added challenge: the dog has to become accustomed to the weight of the material as he powers his way through. He needs lots of encouragement, and plenty of repetitions and rewards, so that he builds up a positive association with this piece of equipment.

As with all aspects of agility, safety is of paramount importance, so the collapsible tunnel should only be attempted with the help of an experienced assistant in addition to your training partner. Take your time with all these exercises, and do not move on unless your dog is completely comfortable with what he is doing.

EXERCISE 47

The collapsible tunnel should be trained as a separate piece of equipment so nothing else is required for this exercise and those that follow.

Initially, the tunnel is held open so the dog has an easy exit.

- Start with step one of the trilogy of learning, with the training partner (T) restraining the dog at the entrance to the tunnel. The assistant (A) stands at the end of the tunnel, pulling it taut so the dog has a clear run through. The handler (H), with toy or treat in hand, is at the exit, ready to reward the dog the second he emerges.

EXERCISE 48

Once your dog has run through a clear tunnel (with the fabric held taut) a couple of times, you can move on to step two of the trilogy with the handler (H) restraining the dog at the mouth of the tunnel, and the training partner (T) standing at the exit. Despite the difference between a flat and a rigid tunnel, most handlers use the same verbal cue, e.g. "tunnel" for both pieces of equipment.

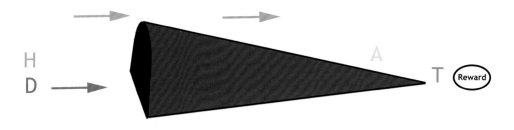

- Repeat the exercise, but this time the assistant lowers the fabric when the dog is nearing the tunnel exit. This gets the dog used to the feeling of the material and he will need extra impetus to find his way out of the tunnel. This can be quite daunting, so the handler should use lots of verbal encouragement; the reward should be high quality treats or an extended game with a favourite toy.
- The smaller your dog, the more you will need to repeat this exercise, as the weight of the tunnel will have greater significance.

What if... Your dog goes through so slowly he is struggling to lift the cloth?

- Make sure your dog knows there is a high value toy or treat at the tunnel exit.
- Give lots of verbal encouragement as he goes through the tunnel.
- Reward at ground level so your dog is looking downwards rather than upwards for his reward. This is much safer and reduces the risk of injury.

EXERCISE 49

When your dog is having 100 per cent success rate with the previous exercise and is powering through the tunnel with confidence, he is ready to find his own way through without the assistant's help.

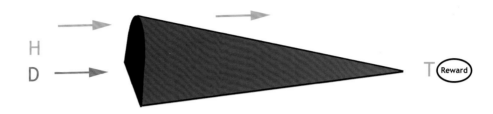

- The handler (H) releases the dog (D) at the tunnel entrance and the training partner (T) is ready to reward at the end of the tunnel.
- The handler runs alongside the tunnel, giving lots of verbal encouragement. The training partner rewards, but the handler should catch up as quickly as possible to give additional treats or continue the game.
- You are asking a lot from your dog, so make sure the reward is really worth working for. You need to boost your dog's confidence so he is thinking about the reward rather than worrying about finding his way through the tunnel.

EXERCISE 50

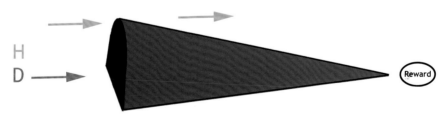

- When – and only when – your dog is completing Exercise 49 with total confidence, you can progress to step three of the trilogy where the dog has to run to his reward without the help of the training partner.

The dog needs to power out of the collapsible tunnel, looking for the next obstacle.

- Now repeat the exercise with the handler running on the other side.
- When your dog is negotiating the collapsible tunnel with confidence, you can add a jump before and after. This teaches him to find the entrance of the tunnel and to drive towards the next obstacle as he emerges.

WHEN SHOULD I END A TRAINING SESSION?

The temptation is to carry on training until you and your dog have got the exercise right. Understandably you are looking for proof that your dog has understood the lesson, and you want to end the session on a good, positive note. But you need to be careful – you may be doing more harm than good.

At its most basic level, agility is all about speed, so you don't want to push your dog to a point where he physically slows down, or learns to pace himself because he anticipates a long, hard training session. Training should always be fun. If your dog is enjoying a positive experience, with lots of rewards, he will keep on learning. If he becomes over-tired or stressed, he will show his feelings by:

• Panting
• Lying down between attempts
• Being slow to re-engage
• Sniffing, scratching, and other forms of distraction behaviour
• Toileting – this may be marking (mostly male dogs) or, in a more extreme case, a dog may empty his bowels. This is undoubtably a sign of stress and may well be a throwback to ancestral flight behaviour.

It is your job to tune into your dog so that you end a training session before you see any signs of this type of behaviour.

WALK BACK

This is a simple exercise which involves asking your dog to walk backwards, in a straight line, on cue.

Walking back teaches an agility dog to co-ordinate and engage his rear end. He has no real need to do this in everyday life but in agility he needs to go into the two-on two-off position when he is negotiating contact equipment (see page 98). He will also need to check his pace and shift his weight to his hindquarters when he goes into the weaves (see page 122). If a dog has a 'walk back' in his repertoire, it will strengthen his muscles and build up the muscle memory so he can do these moves with minimum effort, as well as reducing the risk of injury. Dogs see the 'walk back' as a fun exercise which means it can be used as a way of focusing your dog's attention or it can become part of your start-line routine.

EXERCISE 51
- Start with a treat in your hand and get the dog to focus on it, holding it in front of his nose.
- Using the treat as a lure, move it downwards so the dog's nose is tight to his chest.
- Now place your forefinger on his chest and apply gentle pressure to encourage him to move back.
- Reward any backwards movement, even if he does no more than step back with one back leg.
- Keep practising, asking for a little more before giving the reward.
- In this exercise, less is more, so keep rewarding a stride at a time.

WHAT IF... Your dog goes into a 'sit' instead of walking backwards?
- An obvious one – but make sure you start this exercise with your dog in the 'stand'.
- Your treats may be too tasty, so your dog keeps offering a 'sit' in the hope of getting a reward. Try again with some kibble, which still acts as a reward but should improve your dog's concentration.
- If he keeps trying to sit, encourage him to walk forwards a few paces, following the treat.

Then ask again, using your finger on his chest to encourage backwards movement. The momentum of going forward and then easing him back should prompt him to rock back a stride.

- Reward instantly for any backwards movement, no matter how small.

EXERCISE 52

- Repeat Exercise 51, but phase out the use of your finger to encourage backwards movement. At this stage, you should also be phasing out the treat as a lure, but be ready to reward him as soon as he has walked back a couple of paces.
- Build up the number paces of 'walk back' before rewarding your dog.
- You are now ready to introduce a verbal cue, e.g. "back".

WHAT IF... Your dog is struggling to keep on a straight line when he walks backwards?

It could be that you are asking for too much, too soon. But to assist learning, make it easier by working on this exercise alongside a wall, along a corridor or going down a channel of jump wings. The limited space will help to keep your dog on the straight and narrow...

Agility is a demanding sport so you will need to build up core strength and stability.

KEEPING FIT

The agility dog needs both speed and strength, and keeping your dog fit not only enhances his performance, it also minimises the risk of injury. To keep your dog in peak condition, follow these guidelines:

- Make sure your dog is at the correct weight for his size.
- Adopt a programme of varied exercise to build up endurance and to avoid the physical stresses involved in over-training with agility equipment.
- Jogging with your dog is a great way for you both to keep fit. It is worth investing in the equipment used in Canicross which makes it safer and more comfortable for both dog and handler – who knows you might even take up the sport.
- Use the 'walk back' exercise and other exercises to improve your dog's flexibility, core strength and proprioception (the ability to sense the position, location, orientation and movement of the body and its parts). All will be needed when he is working at speed in agility.
- Start your training session with warm up exercises, and finish with a cool down session. Bear in mind that your dog is prone to injury if he is not fully warmed up.

Denise Fenzi says...

Welcome to dog sports! Agility is an awesome sport, and it's even more awesome when the excitement is equally shared by both halves of the team!

As you start each training session you may want to ask yourself, "Am I having fun? Is my dog having fun?" "Are we enjoying this sport that we are doing together as a team?"

Continue to ask yourself these questions throughout your training session, until it becomes second nature to check in on your mutual enthusiasm for the training process.

All experienced trainers will tell you that working with an excited and engaged partner makes training incredibly easy, whereas working with an unwilling, distracted or sullen partner is bound for failure. Creating a wonderful training atmosphere is the handler's responsibility; find that joy right from the start of your training career! Make it a personal goal never to work with your dog when you're not BOTH equally excited about the tasks in front of you. As you try out each new training technique, check in with your dog. If his eyes are bright and his tail is wagging then you're on the right track; keep going!

If you ever have a doubt about your dog's desire to work with you, stop what you are doing and re-group. Some days that might mean ending training before you're barely begun which can be quite frustrating for the handler! Take that lost time to try and

Trainer's Tip

understand what might have happened to cause your dog to opt out of the training game. Once you have some possible causes, it's time to explore solutions. Other days your dog will be dragging you out of the car and on to the field; wonderful! What caused that reaction? How can you take advantage of that in the future?

At the end of the day, there are no "right" training techniques or "right" ways to do things. There is only what works for you and your dog, and whatever team you can create with each other. Find what works for both of you by asking those same questions over and over, because one thing that should be non-negotiable in your training with your dog is mutual joy.

Remember: Am I having fun? Is my dog having fun? Are we enjoying this sport that we are doing together?

Each time you answer "yes", you will leave that session with a better friend than before you started, and you will begin to truly understand what dog trainers mean when they say they have a relationship with their dog. The ribbons will follow.

TOUCH IT

Tackling contact equipment – the dog-walk, the A-frame and the seesaw – requires speed, balance and accuracy. Safety is a top priority so there is a marked contact area at the start and end of each piece of equipment to ensure the dog goes on straight and, more importantly, does not leap off before he has reached the end.

In the initial stages, you do not need contact equipment. You will be teaching your dog to touch a contact disc, and the correct stop position – two-on two-off (see page 98) – can be taught using a step, a plank, a raised box or you can buy a contact trainer which is made specifically for this purpose.

EXERCISE 53

To get started, you need to teach your dog a hand-touch. This, and the following exercise, can be taught at home, and then transferred to different places to cement your dog's learning.

- Hold your right hand steady with palm outstretched. You will need a treat in your left hand.
- Wait for your dog to touch your right hand with his nose. You can encourage him verbally – "what is it?" – but don't thrust your hand near his face. He needs to make the decision to touch your hand.
- The moment he touches your hand with his nose, transfer the treat from your left hand to your right hand and reward him. It is important that he is always rewarded from the hand he has touched to clarify what he needs to do and to build value for it. When the dog understands the exercise, add a verbal cue: "touch".
- Build on the exercise by moving your hand higher and then lower to the ground so he hand-touches regardless of the position.
- You also need to increase duration. When your dog is responding to the verbal cue "touch", delay rewarding him so he has to keep his nose pressed against your hand for a little longer before he gets a reward.

WHAT IF... Your dog shows no interest in touching your hand?

- Rub a treat on to the palm of your hand and then try – few dogs will resist that enticing smell!

Training with a touch disc teaches a dog to stop at the end of the contact equipment.

- Make your hand more interesting by putting it behind your back and then re-presenting it. Remember not to push your hand towards the dog – he needs to come to you.

EXERCISE 54

You now need to transfer Exercise 53 to a touch disc. This can be anything that is flat and visible, such as the lid of a margarine tub or a jam-jar lid.

- Place the lid in the palm of your right hand, securing it with your thumb. You will need a treat in your left hand.
- Ask your dog to "touch"; the moment his nose touches the lid, reward him by putting a treat on the lid. Rewarding from the lid will help to reinforce the behaviour, which means he is more likely to repeat it.
- Repeat the exercise with your hand holding the disc changing position until you can put the lid on the floor and ask your dog to "touch."
- Practise in different locations so your dog focuses, regardless of other distractions.
- When your dog is achieving a good success rate with this exercise, build duration. On a random basis, delay giving him the treat, or ask him to "touch" a couple of times before rewarding him.
- Building up the 'touch' in this way will ultimately encourage your dog to stay in position on the contact.

EXERCISE 55

The next stage is to teach your dog the two-on two off position, which means he will stop at the end of the contact rather than leaping off it. This involves the dog having his back feet on the contact and his front feet on the ground. For the sake of consistency, he needs to learn to stop in this position every time he hits the end of a contact, regardless of whether it is the dog-walk, the A-frame or the seesaw.

We humans recognise the contact area by its colour, but this isn't going to work for a dog. He needs the change of surface – from the contact to the ground – to tell him he is in the correct position. This can be done by using the touch disc as a training aid.

You don't need contact equipment to teach this exercise. As already stated, you can train on a step, a plank, a raised box or a custom-made contact trainer – anything will do as long as it stands securely on the ground and allows the dog's back end to be positioned higher than his front.

- Place the touch disc at the bottom of the step (or whatever you are using). The dog should be on-lead, and you should have a treat ready in your other hand.

- Now you have to multi-task. Encourage your dog to go on the obstacle and position him so that he sees the touch disc. He knows that if he touches the disc he will get a treat, so he will try to get himself in a position to do this. With a little help from you, he will discover that having his back legs on the step and his front feet on the ground is the easiest way to reach the touch disc.
- Use the lead to keep him position and then ask him to "touch". The moment his nose touches the lid, reward him by putting a treat on the lid.
- Keep practising until your dog goes into the two-on two off position without needing help from you.
- Now ask for several touches so he maintains his position for a longer period.

With practice, your dog will be able work off-lead when he is doing his nose touches.

DOING THE DOG-WALK

You and your dog are now ready to tackle the contact equipment. As your training progresses, you will need access to full scale equipment which is available to hire at various venues. The dog-walk and the A-frame are broadly similar in terms of what you are asking your dog to do. I prefer to start with the dog-walk because it is both narrow and raised, so the dog needs to learn to balance.

Once he has mastered the dog-walk, the A-frame should follow on naturally. The seesaw should be regarded as a completely different piece of equipment and I would not start training it until a dog is completely confident on both the dog-walk and the A-frame. For seesaw exercises, see page 112.

EXERCISE 56
You will be working with the down-plank of the dog-walk which should be propped on a low trestle, just off ground level.

- The training partner scatters treats along the length of the plank and the handler, with dog on lead, encourages the dog to walk along the length of the plank, finding the treats. This will get him used to the surface of the dog walk, and he will need to keep his balance as he walks along the plank.

This is a straightforward exercise so you will be able to move on after a couple of repetitions. Bear in mind that large dogs, and more excitable dogs, find this exercise challenging, so keep everything calm and proceed at a steady pace – speed can come later.

EXERCISE 57
The touch disc is now positioned approximately 10 cm (4in) from the end of the down-plank. You will need to experiment with this depending on the size of your dog, but he needs to be able to reach his touch disc without feeling cramped or needing to stretch. Jump wings

With touch disc training, the dog will learn to focus forwards as he comes down the dog-walk – and he also has a reason to stop!

should be positioned at the bottom of the plank, on either side, which will help to guide the dog into position and prevent him jumping off the side.

- Starting from halfway along the plank, the handler encourages the dog, who is on-lead, to get on to the plank and walk to the end.
- The handler uses the lead to hold the dog gently in the correct two-on two-off position and then asks him to "touch" his disc. The training partner is standing by ready to place a treat on the lid as soon as the dog's nose touches the lid. Always reward from the lid – never from the hand.
- Build on the exercise by asking the dog to stay in position for longer. Ask him to "touch" and reward, and then ask him a second time.

WHAT IF... Your dog fails to maintain the correct two-on two-off position?

Simply go back to the start and repeat the exercise. This is far more effective than trying to correct the position. It gives your dog a chance to think again – he didn't get a reward so he needs to do something different.

EXERCISE 58

With the dog still on-lead, try the full length of the down-plank. The handler also needs to swap sides so the dog learns to focus ahead regardless of the handler's position. The training partner remains in position by the touch disc, ready to reward, when the dog has adopted the correct position and responded to the verbal cue "touch".

EXERCISE 59

You are now ready to work with your dog off-lead.

- This is quite a major progression in training, so the handler should start the dog halfway along the plank with the training partner at the end, ready to reward the "touch".
- Do not attempt a full plank until the dog is 100 per cent successful on the half plank. He needs to be firing forward, paying no attention to the handler who is running alongside. To cement learning, the handler also needs to swap sides.
- Progress the exercise by increasing duration of the two-on two-off position. Vary the number of nose touches you ask for – up to four times – but reward every touch.
- At this stage the training partner is primarily rewarding so the dog focuses forward rather than sideways, looking for the handler. However, the handler should reward on an occasional basis.

- The handler should adopt different positions when the dog reaches the end of the down-plank – sometimes a little ahead, sometimes hanging back. The dog needs to go into the two-on two-off position independently, regardless of the whereabouts of the handler.

EXERCISE 60

Your dog is stopping in position at the end of the dog-walk – you now need to release him. The touch disc is still positioned at the end of the down-plank, but this time you also need to place a treat pot (with a treat on the lid) or toy approximately 2 metres (6 ft) from the bottom of the dog-walk.

- Repeat Exercise 59 with the dog, off-lead, running the full length of the down-plank and handler running alongside.
- As before, the dog is rewarded at the end of the down-plank by the training partner when he responds to his cue to "touch", but now the handler tells him to "go" and releases him to find the treat pot/toy.

WHAT IF... Your dog goes straight to his treat pot/toy without waiting for his cue to "go"?

- Go back a stage and put the dog on lead so you can hold him in position until you are ready to release him. It may take a few repetitions on-lead until he can be trusted.
- Ask your training partner to 'guard' the toy or treat so the dog cannot self-reward.
- You also need to work at your play control. See Controlling the reward, page 53.

EXERCISE 61

Once your dog is running the full length of the down-plank, adopting the two-on two-off position, nose touching his disc and then being released on the cue "go", you can try him on a full dog-walk. But this must be at low height, balanced on purpose-built trestles. Again, the dog is working off-lead.

- Make it easier by starting the dog halfway, and work backwards until the dog is completing the full length dog-walk. The handler can then introduce a verbal cue, such as "walk", to label the equipment. At this stage of learning, the dog should be focusing forward, intent on reaching his touch disc – and his reward – so he should not be too concerned about negotiating the elevated dog walk.
- When the dog is halfway down the down-plank, the handler gives the verbal cue "touch" to give him plenty of time to put on the brakes and stop.
- As before, the dog is rewarded for the 'touch' by the training partner and is released by the handler, with the verbal cue, "go", to head for his treat pot/toy.

- Swap sides so the dog is focusing forwards, regardless of whether the handler is on his right side or his left side.

EXERCISE 62

If your dog is completing Exercise 61 with a success rate of nine times out of ten, you can progress to a full height dog-walk. Even though you are stepping up the degree of difficulty, do not try this with your dog on-lead. You may think you have more control, but it is very hard not to affect your dog's balance, which could make him worried and unsteady.

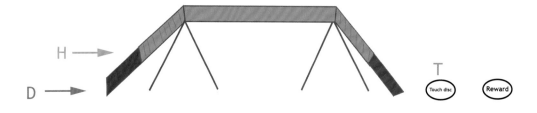

- Use the same set-up with the handler (H) and dog (D) positioned at the the start of the up-plank, and the training partner on hand to reward the "touch".
- The handler releases the dog giving the verbal cue, "walk", and runs alongside.
- As the dog hits the halfway point of the down-plank, the handler gives the cue "touch".
- When the dog assumes the two-on two off position and nose touches his disc, the training partner rewards him. The handler then releases the dog to find his toy/treat pot. You can still use jump wings to help the dog find the correct position at this stage. Only phase them out when the dog is keeping on a straight line.

The final stage of dog-walk training is to phase out the touch disc. See page 120.

WHAT IF... Your dog is worried by the full height of the dog-walk?

- Scatter a treat trail along the full length of the dog-walk so the dog is focusing on finding treats.
- Training partner and handler can walk on either side of the dog to give an added sense of security.
- Go back to using lower trestles so the dog-walk is not at its full height until your dog becomes more confident.

KEEP IT POSITIVE!

Making mistakes is an inevitable part of the learning process – after all, you and your dog are learning together. Even the top handlers don't always get it right!

It is human nature to be disappointed or frustrated when training goes wrong, and we find it very hard to hide our feelings. But this is entirely counter-productive. A dog will learn when he is happy and motivated; he will be very quick to spot any signs of negativity and react accordingly.

Try to follow these guidelines so your training remains focused and positive:

- Keep a check on your body language; your dog is not only picking up information, such as which route he should take, he can also detect whether you are feeling up-beat or downcast. You may think you are masking your frustration, but your dog will read the true story. See Picking up clues, page 138.
- Be careful with your tone of voice; emphatic commands can unnerve a sensitive dog. See Verbal cues, page 77.
- Plan your training sessions, setting realistic goals. See Training Sandwich, page 71.
- Keep your success rate high; your dog should be achieving a success rate of 70 per cent or above before you progress to the next stage of training.
- Observe your dog closely so you do not over-tire him mentally or physically. See When should I end a training session? Page 89.
- Make sure you are offering a reward your dog values, and, if necessary, produce something extra special when you are in a challenging situation. See Before you start, page 12.

TACKLING THE A-FRAME

M ost dogs find the A-frame easier than the dog-walk as it is so much wider, which means that balance and co-ordination are not so much of an issue. However, it is steeper, which means a dog has to approach it with momentum, and he will also find it harder to brake when he reaches the contact area.

EXERCISE 63

Start with the A-frame on its lowest setting which reduces the incline going up and coming down. It is safe to work with your dog on-lead because there is sufficient width, which allows you to guide your dog without affecting his balance.

- The handler encourages the dog on to the A-frame and guides him over it, making sure the lead is held high so it does not get tangled between the dog's legs.
- The touch disc is positioned approximately 10 cm from the end of the A-frame (for an average-sized dog) and the training partner is on standby, ready to reward.
- When the dog is halfway down the A-frame, the handler gives the verbal cue "touch".
- The dog should go into the two-on two-off position, but the handler can use gentle pressure on the lead to control him.
- The training partner rewards as soon as the dog's nose has touched the disc.
- Now repeat the exercise with the handler on the other side.

Practise this exercise and if your dog is negotiating the A-frame with confidence, you can introduce a verbal cue, such as "A" as he goes on to it. The handler should also reduce pressure on the lead so the dog is going into the stop position without assistance.

You want your dog to attack the A-frame with confidence.

WHAT IF... Your dog refuses to go up the A-frame?

- The training partner needs to ensure the dog knows there is a reward at the bottom of the A-frame, and give lots of verbal encouragement. In this instance – for a couple of repetitions only – forget the touch disc and allow the dog to power over the A-frame and be rewarded by the training partner when he reaches the bottom.
- If your dog is still reluctant, lure him with a toy or a treat on the way up; the training partner is then ready to reward as soon as he reaches the contact point. You can then go back and work through Exercise 63.
- Some dogs are concerned about this item of equipment so rather than increasing anxiety, you can lie the A-frame flat on the ground and encourage your dog to walk over it a few times before progressing to the lowest setting.

EXERCISE 64

You are ready to attempt the A-frame with the dog off-lead. But make sure your dog is achieving a good success rate before moving on to this stage.

- The handler needs to swap sides so the dog is happy to tackle the A-frame regardless of which side the handler is on.
- The training partner is ready at the end of the A-frame to reward the nose touch.

EXERCISE 65

You can now increase the height of the A-frame, and gradually progress until your dog is tackling the A-frame at full height; this is a competition requirement regardless of whether your dog is small, medium or large. When you are training, it is not the size of the dog that dictates his progress so much as how confident he feels about tackling the equipment.

- As well as working with the A-frame at full height, the exercise can be progressed by the handler varying position, running ahead or hanging back so the dog finds the stop position on his own.
- Duration for the two-on, two-off position can be built up by increasing nose touches on a random basis, in the region of 1-4, before rewarding.
- Now repeat the exercise with the handler running on the other side of the A-frame.

WHAT IF... Your dog fails to hit the two-on two-off position?

- Guide your dog into the two-on two-off position at the bottom of the contact and give him verbal praise. Then take him back over the whole A-frame so you can reward the correct position.

- If he fails again, go back a stage and put him on-lead. If you need to do this, you should reduce the height of the A-frame so you can guide your dog without affecting his balance.

EXERCISE 66

When your dog is working confidently off-lead, you can add the cue to release him, which means – in the fullness of time – he will be ready to tackle the next obstacle on the course. At this stage, you are releasing to a treat pot/toy so the dog is rewarded for staying in position until he is given his verbal cue. The touch disc remains in place, but a treat pot/toy is now positioned two metres (6 ft) from the bottom of the A-frame.

- The handler (H) releases the dog to go on the A-frame – "A" – and runs alongside as the dog negotiates the obstacle.
- The handler gives the cue "touch" when the dog is halfway down the A-frame.
- The dog is rewarded by the training partner when he hits the two-on two-off position, and touches his disc.
- The handler then tells the dog to "go", releasing him to find his treat pot/toy.

EXERCISE 67

If your dog is achieving a good success rate with Exercise 66 you can add a jump, positioning it approximately 4m (13 ft) from the A-frame.

- The handler (H) positions the dog (D) in front of the jump and asks him to "wait".
- The handler leaves the dog and stands halfway between the jump and the A-frame, with driving arm out-stretched.
- When the dog is released – "OK" – the handler runs alongside as the dog powers over the A-frame and hits his two-on two-off position.
- After responding to the verbal cue, "touch", the dog is rewarded by the training partner (T) before being released to find his treat pot/toy.
- Now repeat the exercise with the handler running on the other side of the A-frame.

To complete your A-frame training, you will need to phase out the touch disc, see page 120.

HOW LONG DOES IT TAKE?

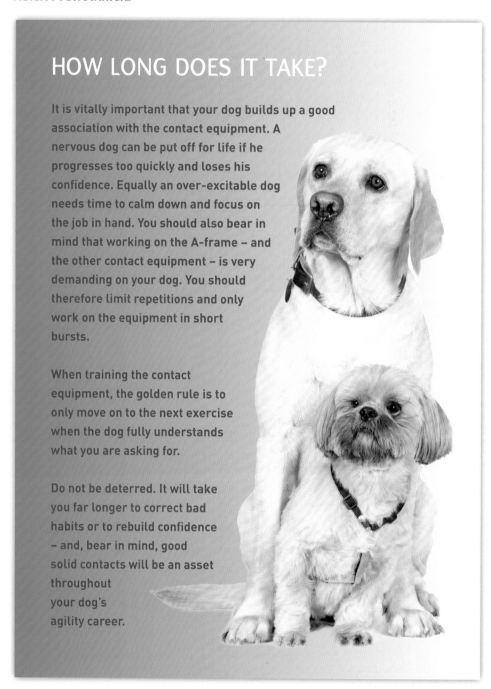

It is vitally important that your dog builds up a good association with the contact equipment. A nervous dog can be put off for life if he progresses too quickly and loses his confidence. Equally an over-excitable dog needs time to calm down and focus on the job in hand. You should also bear in mind that working on the A-frame – and the other contact equipment – is very demanding on your dog. You should therefore limit repetitions and only work on the equipment in short bursts.

When training the contact equipment, the golden rule is to only move on to the next exercise when the dog fully understands what you are asking for.

Do not be deterred. It will take you far longer to correct bad habits or to rebuild confidence – and, bear in mind, good solid contacts will be an asset throughout your dog's agility career.

CHANGING LOCATIONS

When you are training a dog you are communicating with another species. Sometimes this is effortless; at other times you have to stop and work out what is going on in your dog's brain, otherwise confusion and misunderstanding creep in, undermining all your hard work. Understanding a dog's inability to generalise is key to making progress.

For us, it is obvious that if you learn to do something in one location, the fact that you are asked to do it somewhere else makes no odds. Of course, you repeat the same behaviour. But a dog does not follow this thought process. He cannot generalise, and therefore if something changes when he is asked to carry out a training exercise – the environment, the surface, your position – he is no longer sure what you want him to do. He therefore has to go to different places, become accustomed to the handler changing positions, or get used to working on grass if his regular training venue has a sand surface.

When your dog is first learning, you need to take your training to as many different environments as possible so that he learns to ignore change and becomes confident about repeating learned behaviours in new places. Make sure you train with a high-value reward, and make yourself fun and exciting so that he is ready to focus on you. It is a good idea to give your dog a chance to familiarise himself with the new environment before you start training and to start with something relatively straightforward so you can build on success.

TIPPING POINT

The seesaw is the only piece of agility equipment that moves, and it is the only one where the dog has to exert physical control in order to operate it. It should therefore be approached with caution as it can seem both scary and unpredictable.

The rate of progress depends entirely on your dog's level of confidence, but training should never be rushed. If you build up a positive association with this piece of equipment, your dog will have no cause for concern and will think working the tip is all part of the agility game!

EXERCISE 68

The first step in seesaw training is to accustom your dog to standing on an uneven surface. A wobble-board, which can be bought or homemade, is ideal for this purpose as the 'tip' – and therefore the feeling of instability – is minimal.

- Using treats, lure your dog on to the wobble-board and reward him. Initially reward him for putting his front feet on, if he is cautious, and then reward him when he has all four feet on it.
- Be liberal with the treats so your dog is focusing on his rewards rather than worrying about the wobble-board. If your dog is toy orientated, you can have a game of tuggy while he is on the wobble-board.
- Make sure you always reward your dog when he is on the wobble-board.

Watch your dog closely while you are doing this exercise so you can gauge his response. If he is worried, you know that you will have to progress very slowly until he builds up confidence. In all your seesaw training, do not move on to the next stage until your dog is entirely happy with what you are asking him to do.

The dog has to learn operate the seesaw, so training must be broken down into stages.

113

EXERCISE 69

You can now move on to working with a seesaw. Some dogs are more sound sensitive than others and it is not unusual for a dog to be worried by the noise of the seesaw when the plank hits the ground. Seesaws made of aluminium are becoming increasingly common in the ring and these make appreciably more noise than wooden seesaws. So, the next stage in training is to accustom your dog to the sound of the seesaw. For this exercise, you will need a training partner to help you.

- Handler and dog should be working about two metres (6ft) from the seesaw, playing with a toy. For a food orientated dog scatter treats around the seesaw instead.
- As the dog is playing or searching for treats, the training partner keeps pushing the end of the seesaw to the ground.
- As the dog becomes accustomed to the noise of the seesaw, handler and dog can gradually move closer to the seesaw for a food scatter or to play with the toy.
- The dog's reactions needs to be closely monitored. If he is busy with his game or his hunt for treats, you are safe to proceed to the next exercise. If he shows signs of alarm, you need to keep repeating this exercise – extending the radius you are working in and gradually getting closer to the seesaw.
- Watch out for the more subtle signals – yawning, licking, scratching – which indicate stress.

Once your dog has become accustomed to movement of the wobble board, you start training him to go over a mini seesaw (see Exercises 70 and 71).

EXERCISE 70

Now you need to adjust your seesaw to create a mini seesaw. The tip will be greater than the wobble-board, but still minimal. Your dog is now becoming accustomed to the fact not all surfaces he goes on are stable.

- With your dog on-lead, encourage him to go on to the seesaw. This can be from any angle – front, back or side. You are not teaching him to negotiate the seesaw correctly; you are simply getting him used to the unstable surface.
- As soon as he is on the seesaw, reward him with treats or a game. In this way, you are reinforcing the behaviour you want and building up a good association.

EXERCISE 71

Still working with the mini seesaw, you are now training your dog to walk the full length of the seesaw while the training partner controls the tip. For this exercise the dog is on-lead.

- The handler encourages the dog to step on to the seesaw at the start of the up-plank. The training partner stands at the far end, holding the seesaw level. The touch disc is positioned approximately 10cm from the end of the seesaw.
- The dog negotiates the full length of the seesaw with the handler beside him. The lead must be held high to prevent it getting tangled between the dog's legs or affecting his balance.

BEWARE!

From a dog's perspective the start of the seesaw looks the same as the up-plank of the dog-walk. It is therefore easy for him to confuse the two, and he may become wary of the up-plank of the dog-walk, anticipating the tip of the seesaw.

To prevent this happening, it is best to complete your training on one piece of equipment before starting the other. You also need to make sure that your verbal cues for the two pieces of equipment are very clear and sound completely different from each other.

- When the dog reaches the end of the seesaw, the training partner rewards him with a treat/toy.
- The handler takes over feeding or playing with the dog while the training partner gradually lowers the seesaw to the ground.
- As the seesaw reaches ground level, the handler asks the dog to "touch". When he has adopted the two-on two-off position (which he has learnt from his dog-walk and A-frame training) he is rewarded for a second time.

EXERCISE 72

I call this exercise the bang bang game, as the aim is to accustom the dog to the noise and movement of a full size seesaw before attempting to negotiate the whole obstacle.

- The training partner holds the end of the seesaw just above ground level and the handler encourages the dog, on-lead, to jump on to the raised contact area at the end of the seesaw.
- The training partner lets go, allowing the dog's weight to take the seesaw to ground level. At this stage, the tip, and therefore the movement, is minimal but the dog is experiencing what it is like to operate the seesaw. The noise of the seesaw hitting the ground is also very slight.
- As the dog grows in confidence, the training partner holds the seesaw further from the ground so the tip, and the noise of the seesaw hitting the ground, increases.

EXERCISE 73

The dog, who is still on-lead, is now ready to negotiate the seesaw in its entirety. The training partner holds the seesaw so it will not tip until the dog reaches the end.

- At the end point of the seesaw, the handler rewards with toy or treat, and the training partner lowers the seesaw to the ground. The dog then nose-touches the disc and is released.
- After a number of repetitions, the dog will be ready to try the exercise off-lead.
- If all is going well, the training partner can lower the seesaw more quickly allowing it to bang.

WHAT IF... Your dog is scared by the seesaw and tries to jump off?

This is a challenging piece of equipment and you need to monitor your dog's reactions at all stages of training. If he is showing anxiety, you have probably rushed your training, so you will need to go back a stage. Try to work out what is causing him concern: is it the movement, the height or the noise? If you know what is worrying him, you will be able to focus your attention on that area until your dog is comfortable.

The seesaw can be a source of concern to some dogs, so take your time when teaching this piece of equipment.

EXERCISE 74

It is now time to phase out the training partner so the dog must operate the tip of the seesaw independently. However, the training partner is in position at the end of the seesaw to reward the nose touch.

- The handler encourages the dog to go on the seesaw and runs alongside.
- The dog should now understand that he must run to the end and then the seesaw will tip to hit the ground.
- The contact disc is in place ready for the nose touch when the dog hits the two on two off position.
- The training partner's help with the seesaw should be phased out gradually. The dog can do a couple of seesaws, operating the tip independently, and then the training partner can be reintroduced to help with the tip on a random basis. This is particularly important if the dog is showing concern. At this stage, the training partner is always on hand to reward the dog for his nose touch.
- When the dog is operating the seesaw successfully, introduce a verbal cue, such as "see". The cue is delayed until this late stage as the dog needs to have a positive association with this piece of equipment. If it is introduced too early, when the dog may be worried by the noise or the movement, it may have a negative connotation which will be hard to overcome.

This is a very difficult stage and it will take many repetitions before your dog learns the sequence of skills that are required.

EXERCISE 75

You are now ready to release the dog from the seesaw to find his reward after he has completed his nose touch.

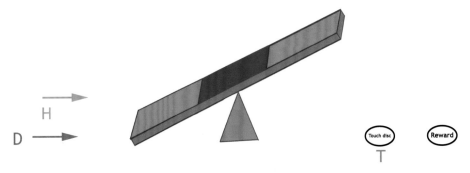

- Repeat Exercise 74 but this time place a toy or treat pot approximately two metres (6 ft) from the end of the seesaw. The contact disc remains in place, 10cm from the end of the seesaw.
- The handler (H) directs the dog (D) to the seesaw – "see" – and runs alongside.
- The dog runs to the end of the seesaw, tips it and then goes into the two-on two-off position for the nose touch and is rewarded by the training partner (T).
- The handler releases him – "go" – and he runs to his toy or treat pot.

To complete your seesaw training, see Phasing out the touch disc, page 120.

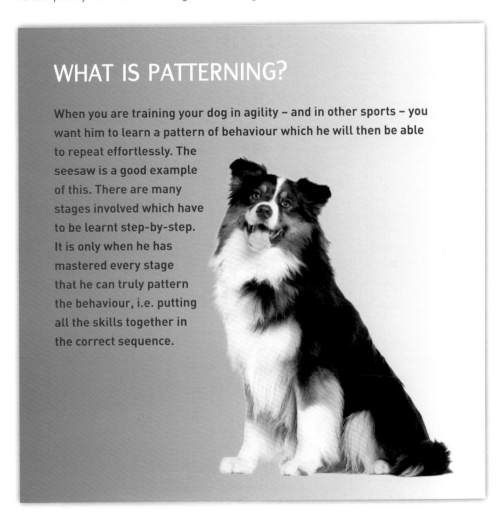

WHAT IS PATTERNING?

When you are training your dog in agility – and in other sports – you want him to learn a pattern of behaviour which he will then be able to repeat effortlessly. The seesaw is a good example of this. There are many stages involved which have to be learnt step-by-step. It is only when he has mastered every stage that he can truly pattern the behaviour, i.e. putting all the skills together in the correct sequence.

PHASING OUT THE TOUCH DISC

The touch disc is a training aid which is used to teach the dog to stop at the end of the contact equipment. It cannot be used in competition and therefore it needs to be phased out so the dog knows what he needs to be doing – going into the two-on two-off position – without the prompt of the touch disc.

You can practise the following exercises at home, when you are out an about, as well as when you are working with agility equipment.

EXERCISE 76
Change your touch disc to a transparent lid (it is not so obvious).
- Place the disc on the ground and ask your dog to "touch" and then reward.
- When your dog has got used to his new touch disc, try it with the contact equipment.

EXERCISE 77
Now cut the lid in half, reducing the size of the target area.
- Ask your dog to "touch" and then reward.
- Now try it with the contact equipment.
- Next withdraw the lid and ask him to "touch". Give him time to work it out, but as he knows that "touch" means nose touch – and the disc has been placed on the ground – he will make the connection. Give him a big reward when he makes the breakthrough.
- Alternate nose touches with and without the disc so your dog realises that he doesn't need the disc to offer the correct behaviour and therefore get his reward.
- Now practise with the contact equipment. This is a gradual process, so start with the disc and then withdraw it. Keep practising using the disc and withdrawing it on a random basis.
- When rewarding, alternate handler and training partner as the training partner needs to be phased out, too.

- Continue working on this until you have achieved a 70 per cent success rate or above.

EXERCISE 78

You can now start phasing out the training partner so that the handler releases the dog to his toy once the nose touches have been completed. At this stage, divide reward-giving so that 50 per cent of the time the dog is rewarded for the nose touch and for the rest of the time he nose touches and is released to his reward. You need to be working on contact equipment.

- The handler cues the dog to go on to the contact equipment – the dog-walk, for example. The training partner is positioned at the end, with a treat or a toy. A second reward (treat pot/toy) is positioned two metres (6 ft) further back.
- The handler, running alongside, asks the dog to "touch" when he is halfway from the bottom of the equipment.
- When the dog stops and nose touches in the two-on two-off position, the training partner steps in and rewards the dog on the contact area.
- The handler releases with a verbal cue – "go" – and the dog goes to find his second reward.
- Repeat, but this time the training partner in not on hand to reward the nose touch. The dog goes into the two-on two-off position on the handler's verbal cue, "touch" and completes his nose touch. He is then released by the handler to find his reward.

What If... Your dog goes directly to his toy?

- You need to go back a few stages and create value for the nose touches by rewarding them.
- You can increase motivation by changing your treats.
- You need to work at your play control, see page 53.
- For a few repetitions, lose the second reward and focus on rewarding the nose touch.

FOR THE TOY-DRIVEN DOG

If your dog is strongly motivated by toys, you can teach him to play when he is on the contact instead of rewarding him with a treat. The advantage of rewarding with a toy is that it increases motivation, and therefore speed. At some competitions you can register to be NFC (not for competition) so you can bring a toy (not treats) into the ring. If you have transferred your training to a toy you will get the opportunity to reward your contacts in the ring.

GET WEAVING

R unning, jumping and balancing – essential skills for the agility dog – come naturally. But weaving is a different matter.

This is something that has to be trained and, unless you build in lots of rewards, it can easily seem like a chore. However, if you break weave training into simple steps, using positive reinforcement, your dog will not only see weaving as fun, he will become a high-speed specialist.

- A full set of weaves is made up of 12 poles positioned in a straight line, with 60cm (2ft) between poles; the minimum height of the poles is 76.2cm (2ft 6in). In competition, the number of poles can range from 5 to 12, but, traditionally, weaves will be in blocks of 6, 9 and 12.
- The dog must enter the weaves with the first pole adjacent to his left shoulder, regardless of which side the handler is on. Faults are accrued for incorrect entry and for failure to complete the full set of weaves.
- There are many different ways to teach a dog to weave. I focus on the 2 x 2 method, invented by world champion agility trainer, Susan Garrett. This method promotes understanding and value for the weave entry, and the process of learning is made simpler for the dog. In addition, I also use channel weaves to boost confidence, therefore encouraging speed and a full commitment to completing the full set of weaves.
- Training your dog to weave is complex, so do not be impatient. It needs frequent repetitions and these need to be done on a regular basis, progressing only when your dog has mastered the previous stage. For this reason, you may decide to buy a set of garden weaves (available via the Internet) so you can practise at home.

2 x 2 WEAVES

Susan Garrett bases all her work on positive reinforcement. Put in basic terms, this means focusing on what you want your dog to do, rather than what you don't want. Her method of 2 x 2 weaving relies on shaping a dog's behaviour – rewarding the behaviour the dog offers, rather than luring or guiding him. She focuses on the first two weave poles, as getting the correct entry is the route to success. You therefore need to build value for the dog in getting this right.

The aim is to build value for getting the correct entry to the weaves.

Below is a brief overview of Susan's 2 x 2 weave training. If you want to train your dog using this method, you will need to watch her DVD, Susan Garrett's *2 x 2 Weave Training*, to clarify your understanding (see Further Information, page 159).

I recommend the 2 x 2 method for all novice dogs. To increase speed and to improve your dog's rhythm and co-ordination through the weaves – especially for large dogs – finish off your weave training by putting them through the Channel Weaves (see page 132).

EXERCISE 79

Imagine a clock face and your two weave poles are placed at 12 and 6. Now pick up the poles and place them at 8 and 2. This makes the entry easier to find.

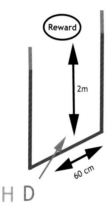

- The handler should spend a few moments playing and interacting with the dog so that he is engaged and ready to work.
- Handler (H) and dog (D) stand alongside the gap between the two poles and the handler is ready to reward any movement towards them – though this may be no more than a glance or a sniff.
- The handler keeps rewarding this, each time waiting for the dog to offer more. When he gets the idea of moving through the two poles, you must reward him instantly.
- The handler must reward the dog in the direction he is moving, i.e. as he is emerging from the second pole.

EXERCISE 80

Once your dog understands that he must find the entry to the weave poles, you need to increase the degree of difficulty.

- Swap sides so the dog has to find the weave entry regardless of the handler's position. Position him at different angles so he has to work harder to find the entry.
- Take your weave poles to different places so your dog can apply his new-found knowledge away from home.
- At this stage, do not introduce a verbal cue, e.g. "weave", as your dog is not actually weaving. As he goes through the learning process, there will be lots of errors along the way so you don't want to name the behaviour until it is properly established.

You may wonder why you need to make things more difficult at this early stage. But if your dog learns to find the weave entry from both sides and from all angles, regardless of where you are standing, he will, eventually, have the confidence to weave independently, which is a great asset when you are negotiating a course.

EXERCISE 81

Now move on to working with four poles. Repeat the positioning of the first two poles, allowing a gap of approximately 4.5m (15ft) between the two sets of poles. Again, the handler (H) must keep swapping sides so the dog (D) is finding the entry independently.

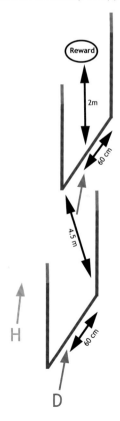

- Wait for your dog to negotiate the first two poles, and then reward him in the gap between the two sets of poles.
- Wait for him to complete the second set of weaves poles, and reward him again.
- After a few repetitions, you can reward when he has completed four poles, but mix it up so you intermittently reward for two poles.
- It is important to retain value for the first set of poles otherwise your dog may try to skip them if he thinks he only gets a reward after the second set.
- Gradually close the gap between the two sets of poles, and change the angle of the weaves until they are in a straight line.
- It is inevitable that your dog will make mistakes, but do not reinforce this behaviour by helping him out. Allow him to work out what he has to do – and make a huge fuss of him when he gets it right!

EXERCISE 82

Once your dog is negotiating four weave poles in a straight line, you can add two more. To make it easier, position the first two weaves as a 'gate' positioned at 8 and 2, with the remaining four poles in a straight line.

- Repeat the exercise with the handler swapping sides.
- When your dog is confidently negotiating six poles, close the angle of the first two so all six poles are in a straight line.
- Do not progress until your dog is achieving a success rate of 70 per cent or above.
- Repeat the exercise with the handler swapping sides.

EXERCISE 83

Weave training is an on-going process, so keep practising with the handler swapping sides and the dog finding the entry from a variety of different angles. You can now work with 12 weaves poles, positioned as a set of six poles (in a straight line) a gap of 3.5 to 4.5m (12-15 ft), and then six poles in a straight line.

- Gradually decrease the gap between the two sets of weave poles, rewarding in-between. Then you are ready to join the two sets together. Now you can introduce the verbal cue, "weave" – and celebrate the fact that you have a dog who can negotiate a full set of 12 weave poles!

Weaving does not come naturally to a dog – he needs to learn balance and co-ordination as he works his way through 12 poles.

Susan Garrett says...

Placement of reward is incredibly important in training weave poles. In the 2 x 2 training method we have a 'reward line'. This specific line is in the middle of the open poles and between 2m and 3m (6-10 ft) from the end of the poles.

Trainer's Tip

Your reward placement should always be positioned / tossed / thrown and celebrated on this line. When training partners focus on this dog training detail, weave training sessions will go from mediocre to *dynamite!* Focus on your *reward line!*

CHANNEL WEAVES

Once your dog has learnt how to weave, you may find it useful to put him through the channel weaves which help to increase motivation, speed and co-ordination. This method of weave training involves opening a channel between two lines of weave poles, and then gradually narrowing it until your dog is weaving in a straight line.

EXERCISE 84

For this, you need 12 weave poles. Place six in a straight line, 120cm (4ft) apart. Then set up a second line, leaving just a metre's width (3ft) between the two sets of weave poles. The first pole is placed opposite the first line of poles, at the midway point between poles 1 and 2. The remaining five poles are placed at 120cm intervals. Start with stage two of the trilogy, with the training partner ready to reward at the end of the exercise.

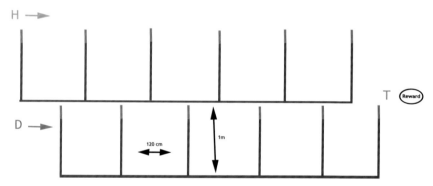

- Remember, the dog must enter the weaves with his left shoulder adjacent to the first pole, so as you look down the two lines of poles, the pole nearest you should be on the left.
- The handler (H) restrains the dog (D) at the entry point and the training partner (T) is positioned at the end of the weaves with a toy or treat.
- The handler releases the dog and the training partner calls him down the channel, rewarding him as soon as he has reached the exit.
- In all weave training, the handler needs to swap sides so the dog finds the entry regardless of the handler's position.

WHAT IF... Your dog ducks out of the weave channel and heads straight for his reward?

- In the short term, the training partner can 'guard' the reward until the dog has reached the end of the channel.

The training partner makes the reward obvious so the dog heads straight down the weave channel.

As training progresses, the training partner is taken out of the equation and the dog must head for his reward without assistance.

- In the long term, work on your toy/treat control. The best way of doing this is to take your lesson away from agility equipment and practise calling your dog away from his reward (see Controlling the reward, page 53).

EXERCISE 85

Repeat Exercise 84, but now you have moved the weaves to create a narrower channel.

- The handler (H) releases the dog (D) who powers down the channel to be rewarded by the training partner (T).
- Keep narrowing the weave channel in tiny stages, only progressing when your dog is powering through to the end.

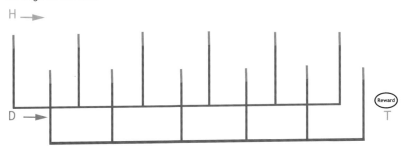

- The weave channel is becoming progressively narrower so the dog needs to change his body movement to head down the channel.
- If the dog (D) is maintaining a high success rate, phase out the training partner so the dog must find the reward without assistance. However, if he starts to come out of the weave channel, go back a stage so the training partner 'guards' the reward until he has completed the exercise.
- Throughout training, the handler should keep swapping sides and changing angles so the dog has to find the entry independently.
- Add a jump before the weaves so the dog has to adjust his stride and slow down in order to hit the correct point of entry.
- As the channel narrows, the dog will be learning how to co-ordinate his body so that he is effectively 'weaving' before the poles are in a straight line.

EXERCISE 86

When the dog is achieving a 70 per cent or above success rate on the narrowest of channels, you can position the poles in a straight line.

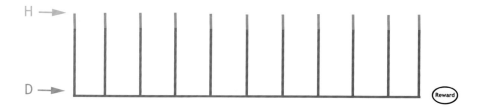

As already emphasised, this is a complex exercise and you should not be concerned about going back a stage in order to clarify understanding. When you are confident that your dog understands what is required, introduce the verbal cue "weave".

- Weave training must take place on both sides so the handler (H) starts with the dog (D) on the right and asks him to "weave".
- The handler now swaps sides so the dog is finding the weave entry from the other side.

WHAT IF... *Your dog is struggling and keeps coming out of the weaves?*

- Graduating to a straight line of weaves may seem minimal to you in terms of closing the gap, but the line of poles will appear quite different to your dog, and he may find the final transition difficult.
- The rule of thumb is, if your dog comes out of the weaves more than three times, go back a stage and make the channel wider.

DON'T BE AN AIMLESS TRAINING PARTNER

If you are working with your dog on your own, it is very easy to lose direction and to carry on for too long, running the risk of your dog losing speed and motivation. What can you do to prevent this?

- Plan your session, allocating approximately five minutes for an exercise.
- Set a timer so you know when the five minutes are up.
- Decide in advance on the number of repetitions you want when teaching an exercise and do not exceed it – even if your dog makes a mistake on the last one.
- Take a break. If you allow your dog to relax for 5 or 10 minutes, he will be more ready to learn.
- If your dog has been awesome – finish early!

Remember, you also need to be in the right frame of mind. If you are tired or preoccupied, or simply lacking motivation yourself, forget it. Your dog will be very quick to sense your mood and the training session is unlikely to be fruitful.

IT'S A WRAP

In the early days of agility, dogs and handlers worked pretty much in a circle, with the dog staying on one side. Now the sport is much more challenging and courses, particularly at the higher levels, are full of twists and turns. As a handler, your job is to open up the fastest line for you and your dog.

To do this you need to teach your dog to follow your driving arm and read your body language so he knows which way to go. Clarity and timing are the vital ingredients in handling, so both you and your dog will be learning together.

When I am training new handlers I start with wing work – teaching the dog to wrap around a wing – as this is relatively straightforward and encourages the dog to check his stride and turn as tightly as possible.

EXERCISE 87

For this exercise you can use a single jump wing, but if you don't have agility equipment you can use a stool, a chair or a plant pot – any obstacle will do as long as it does not look like a weave pole.

- The handler has a treat in both hands, and the dog starts on the left-hand side, positioned next to a jump wing.
- Using the treat in the left hand, the handler lures the dog around the wing in a clockwise direction.
- When the dog has completed the circle, the handler rewards using the treat from the right hand.
- Keep practising, decreasing the help the dog needs. The handler no longer needs a treat in the left hand to lure the dog; the reward is given from the right hand as soon as the dog has come round the wing.
- At the stage, the handler can use a verbal cue, such as "wrap", and transfer from using treats to a toy if this is the dog's preferred reward.

EXERCISE 88

- Repeat Exercise 87, but this time the dog is positioned on the handler's right-hand side and is lured around the wing in an anti-clockwise direction. The dog is rewarded from the left-hand side. The verbal cue, "wrap" is used, regardless of which side the dog is working on.
- From now on, work on both the left-hand side and right-hand side in equal measure.
- The reason you reward from the opposite hand is because you are picking the dog up from this side when he has completed the wrap, ready to move on to the next part of the course. You need to give value to the new drive arm, reinforcing what side you want your dog to be on.

EXERCISE 89

You are still practising the wing wrap in both directions, but you are ready to increase the distance the dog must cover to reach the wing. In a course, this extra flexibility allows the dog to work ahead of you, and allows you to get to a new position while your dog is wrapping round the wing. This exercise should be taught in stages, gradually building up the distance.

- The handler is positioned by a cone approximately one metre (3ft) from the jump wing. The handler sends the dog, with arm signal and verbal cue, to find the wing and wrap round it.

The aim is to get your dog to wrap tightly around the wing.

- The handler moves off as the dog is wrapping round the wing so the dog has to speed up as he completes the wrap to rejoin the handler and get his reward.
- Keep practising, moving the cone further back until the handler can stand approximately two metres from the jump wing.

WHAT IF... Your dog doesn't want to go round the wing when he is sent from a distance?

- The dog may be struggling because you are holding the toy/treat ready to reward him so ask your training partner to step in and reward by the wing. This will increase value for the wing rather than the handler.

EXERCISE 90

You are now working with two jump wings placed 5m (16ft) apart, and sending the dog to wrap round both wings in a figure of eight. You can also use cones, which gives you the opportunity to train this exercise in different locations (see Changing locations, page 111).

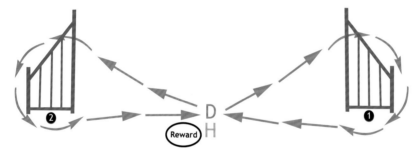

- The handler (H) stands between two jump wings with the dog (D) on the left-hand side.
- On the verbal cue "wrap", the dog is sent round jump wing 1, guided by the handler's left arm, in a clockwise direction.
- The handler picks him up on the right arm and sends him to wrap around jump wing 2 in an anti-clockwise direction.
- When the dog has completed the second wrap, the handler rewards with the left hand.
- Try the exercise again with the dog starting on the handler's right-hand side.

EXERCISE 91

You can now work with a single jump, with the pole at the the lowest height.

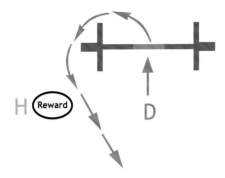

- The handler (H) stands in front of the jump with the dog (D) on right-hand side.
- On the verbal cue, "wrap", the handler uses his right arm to direct the dog towards the jump and to circle the left wing.
- The handler picks him up on his left arm and rewards.
- Now repeat the exercise swapping sides so the dog starts on the handler's left-hand side and wraps around the right jump wing.

EXERCISE 92

To progress your wrap training, position two jumps approximately approximately 4m (13ft) apart.

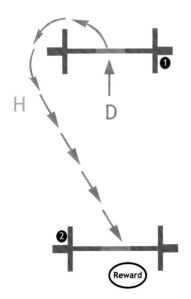

- The handler (H) stands in front of the jump with the dog (D) on the right-hand side.
- On the verbal cue, "wrap', the handler uses his right arm to direct the dog towards the jump and to circle the left wing.
- Now repeat the exercise with the dog starting on the left of the handler and wrapping round the right wing.

PICKING UP CLUES

We humans communicate first and foremost through language, and therefore we think that giving dogs verbal cues is a top priority.

Dogs do learn to pick up on what we say – but they are far more focused on what we do. Dogs communicate by reading each other's body language, and your dog will find your body – your signals, your stance, and your positioning – is far more informative than anything you say.

In agility, more than any of the other dog sports, you need to be aware of what you are doing physically as this gives vital information about where you want your dog to go. He will listen to your directional cues – "left" or "right" – but the position of your driving arm, and whether you are turning your shoulders left or right, will have far greater significance.

With practice you will be able to fine tune your handling skills, eliminating the muddle and the grey areas. Your highly intelligent dog will then be able to pick up the most subtle of clues, at lightening speed, giving him a winning advantage as he negotiates an agility course.

EXERCISE 93

Now your dog has learnt to wrap around a wing, you can put the move into a short sequence.

For this exercise you will need a tunnel and three jumps.

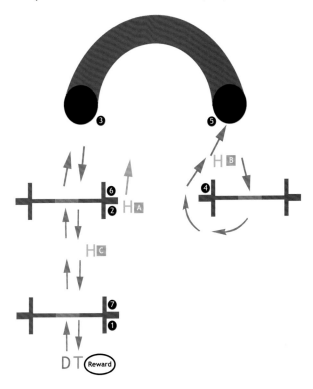

- Starting with the dog on the left-hand side, the handler (Hᴀ) guides him over jumps 1 and 2 and then into the tunnel (3).
- As the dog emerges from the tunnel, the handler (Hʙ) stands in front of jump 4, and using his left arm, asks the dog to "wrap".
- The handler then sends the dog back into the tunnel (5) using their right arm as the driving arm.
- When the dog is committed to the tunnel the handler moves to position Hc to pick up the dog (with the right drive arm) and guides him over jumps 6 and 7 where he is rewarded by the training partner (T).

Silvia Trkman says...

Cik & cap turns (also known as wing wraps) are a great asset in agility, and they are born out of a trick. That's where the name comes from: cik-cap/zig-zag is what I called a figure-of-eight with the dog going through my legs.

I then generalised the trick by sending the dog to wrap other objects, like trees and poles, then jump wings – and then eventually jump wings with a bar in between.
I started on the lowest height and then placed the pole higher and higher. I discovered that this was a very easy, elegant way to cut two to five seconds from course times and, at the same time, training sends, turns, distance skills, independence, commitment and obstacle focus.

When you are first starting in agility, both dog and handler have so much more to learn. But, by using cik & cap, your dog will have the confidence to run and have fun in the early stages of training. It also allows you, the handler, to have more time to think about where and how to cross when you are running a course.

Clear handling and accurate timing are easier to achieve with cik & cap, as it allows you to get a perfect turn even when you don't happen to be on the perfect spot at the

Trainer's Tip

perfect moment. And probably most importantly, it allows the dog to know where he is going next so that he has time to adjust his speed and prepare for the turn, which reduces the physical stress on his joints.

So yes, cik & cap is definitely the trick that you want to teach to every agility dog. You can shape it with a clicker, but you can as easily lure it, name it, and then use it on daily walks with trees, progressing to the agility field. I am sure it will make a big difference!

CHANGING SIDES

I n order to handle your dog around an agility course, you need to open up lines which give you the quickest route while showing your dog which obstacle he should take.

To achieve this, you need to continually change sides so you can handle on either your dog's left side or right side. At their most basic level these moves, known as handling points, can be be divided into a Front Cross, which takes place ahead of the dog and a Rear Cross, which involves the handler working behind the dog.

FRONT CROSS

This relies on your ability to get ahead of your dog, and is generally used by handlers who can run fast or those who can send their dog ahead, allowing them to get in position for a front cross. The moves involve the handler completing a 180 degree turn which will enable the dog to change sides.

EXERCISE 94

Executing a handling point successfully is all about getting your timing right, and this needs to be practised by both dog and handler. I teach this exercise using five jumps, set on their lowest height. It is easier if the training partner restrains your dog so you have plenty of time to get into the best position to start the exercise.

- Dog (D) and training partner (T) are in front of jump 1 with the dog on the right-hand side. The handler (HA) stands between jumps 2 and 3.
- The training partner releases the dog and the handler picks him up on his right (driving) arm to show him jumps 1 and 2.
- As the dog approaches jump 2, the handler in position HB turns to the right to face the dog, switching between right and left arm while completing the turn, so the handler is facing jump 3. The dog is now committed to the left arm – the new driving arm – and the right arm drops out of the equation.

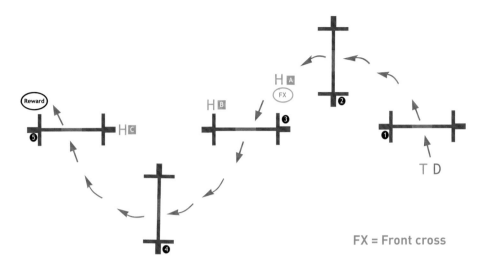

FX = Front cross

- For the first few repetitions, the handler should hold a toy or treat in their left hand, ready to reward the dog for changing on to the left side. This reinforces that this is the new driving arm, and the side the dog should now be working on.
- The dog is guided by the left arm and takes jumps 3, 4 and 5 to find his reward at the end of the course.

Getting into the correct position is all important for the front cross.

143

EXERCISE 95

Looking at the line drawing (below), the dog is working on the handler's right-hand side as he works his way round the course, and emerges from the tunnel. However, if he stayed on the right side to go over jumps 5 and 6, there would be nothing to indicate the whereabouts of jump 7. Therefore, the handler needs to change sides between jumps 4 and 5 by putting in a front cross. This point marks the change of direction and, by changing sides, the handler opens up a new line for the dog to take. He will now be working on the handler's left side, taking a direct route to jumps 5, 6, and 7. Depending on your stage of training, you can ask your training partner to restrain the dog at the start for a couple of repetitions and then try a 'wait'.

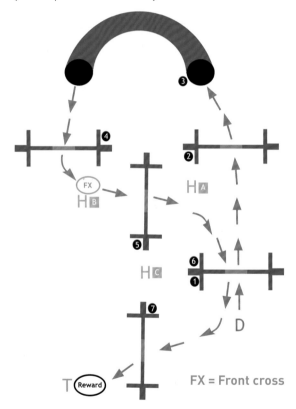

FX = Front cross

- The handler (HA) recalls the dog over jump 1, with the dog working on the right side.
- After jump 2, the handler sends the dog to the tunnel, and moves into position at the midway point between jumps 4 and 5.

- With the right arm out-stretched, pointing towards where the dog is coming from, the handler (HB) waits for the dog to emerge from the tunnel.
- Once the dog exits the tunnel, the handler starts the front cross, turning their body to the right (to face the direction the dog is coming from), smoothly changing from right arm out-stretched to left arm out-stretched while rotating to point at jump 5.
- For the first few repetitions the handler rewards the dog with a toy or treat, using the left hand, to give value to the change of direction.
- The handler, at position Hc, guides to the dog over jumps 6 and 7 to find his reward at the end of the course.

EXERCISE 96

Repeat Exercise 95 but this time, working with your dog on the left-hand side, and doing your front cross between jumps 4 and 5. At this point, the reward, placed after jump 7, is in your dog's eye-line so ask your training partner to guard it until you have completed the front turn.

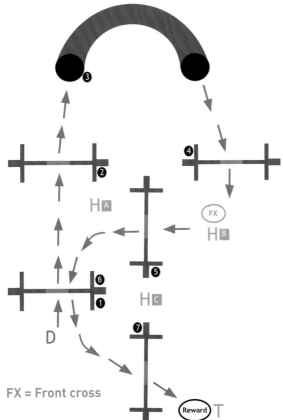

FX = Front cross

WHAT IF... You can't get between jumps 4 and 5 in time?

- You need to do more work on your dog's tunnel drive so that he will send to the tunnel independently while you move into position (see Go tunnel, page 22).
- You may be dog watching – hanging around by the tunnel entrance to ensure your dog goes in rather than moving into position.

REAR CROSS

As the name implies, this move takes place behind the dog. This means that as the dog takes the jump, the handler crosses behind to switch sides. In some ways this is harder than the front cross – for the dog, at least – as he has to take the equipment that lies ahead of the handler.

EXERCISE 97

The easiest way to practise a rear cross is going into a tunnel, as this is a natural draw for most dogs and will encourage forward focus (see page 28).

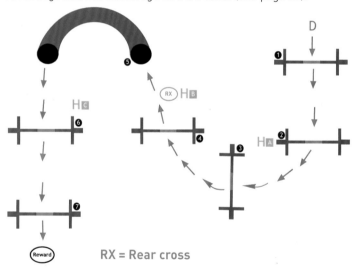

RX = Rear cross

- The handler (Hᴀ) recalls the dog over jump 1 and, with the dog on the left side, takes him around the fan and heads towards the tunnel.
- The rear cross takes place at the midway point between jump 4 and the tunnel entrance.
- When the dog is a stride away from the tunnel, the handler (Hʙ) changes arms so that the right arm is now driving at the tunnel. This will help the dog to change lead leg and he will know which arm to look for when he comes out of the tunnel.
- Once the dog is in the tunnel, the handler crosses behind the dog and is in position (Hc) to use his new driving arm – the right arm – to take the dog over jumps 6 and 7.

Rear crossing relies on good timing.

EXERCISE 98

Now try the rear cross, with a jump. This is harder for the dog as he has to change direction after the jump. He must therefore have a good understanding of his directionals and the verbal cues you use. You can practise this with a single jump on its lowest height.

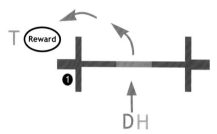

- Dog and handler (H) start before the jump, with the dog on the handler's left-hand side. The training partner (T) is positioned to the left of the jump with toy or treat.
- The handler (H) sends the dog towards the jump using their left arm, and while giving the verbal cue "left", smoothly changes to the right arm to show the dog where to go next. The left arm drops out of the equation. The training partner (T) is ready to reward when the dog takes the jump and turns to the left.

EXERCISE 99

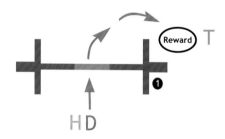

- Repeat Exercise 98 but this time change direction.
- Start with the dog on the right-hand side (H) and the training partner (T) positioned ready to reward when the dog has taken the jump.
- This time the verbal cue is, "right", and the training partner rewards as the dog lands, turning towards the right.
- As the dog becomes more experienced, and your timing improves, he will start turning in the correct direction while he is in the air.

EXERCISE 100

You are now ready to try the rear cross within a sequence of jumps. The rear cross takes place between jumps 4 and 5 which is just before the change of direction and, therefore, where the handler needs to swap sides.

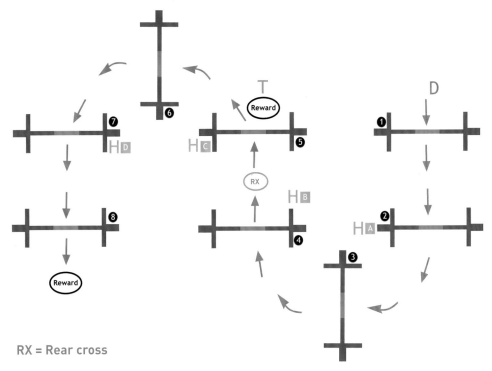

RX = Rear cross

- Starting with the dog (D) on the left-hand side, the handler (Hᴀ) uses his driving arm – the left arm – to take the dog over jumps 1, 2, 3 and 4.
- Just before the dog takes jump 5, the handler (Hʙ) smoothly changes arms from left to right. The verbal verbal cue "go" is used to encourage the dog to take the jump, followed by a directional – in this case "left" – to indicate the direction he must move in to take the remaining jumps.
- To facilitate learning, the training partner (T) stands behind jump 5 ready to reward the rear cross.
- The handler, now at position Hc, continues round the course to Hᴅ, using his right arm as his drive arm. The dog takes jumps 6, 7, and 8 and runs on to find his reward.

WHAT IF... *Your dog fails to take the jump ahead (jump 5 in this instance)?*

• You need to create more value for your dog working independently and taking the obstacle that lies ahead. For a couple of repetitions start in front of jump 5, with the training partner rewarding, before attempting the whole exercise.

WHAT IF... *Your dog takes the jump ahead (jump 5) as you rear cross but spins to the right before taking the next jump (jump 6)?*

• You may not be giving the verbal cue, "left" early enough, but it is more likely that the dog doesn't have a solid understanding of directionals over a jump. You can rectify this by practising exercises 98 and 99.

• You may not be changing arms early enough for your dog to see the change of direction (in this case left to right). It will help if your training partner films you (see page 58).

EXERCISE 101

Once your dog is committed to taking the jump that lies ahead (jump 5), you can try the whole sequence with the training partner ready to reward at the end of the course. Complete the learning process by taking the training partner out of the equation and sending the dog to find his reward.

DECISION MAKING

Whether you decide to change sides with a front or a rear cross often comes down to personal preference. You and your dog may have found one easier than the other, so this may be the handling move you generally choose. Personally, I prefer to front cross as it allows me to stay ahead of my dog and opens up new lines of the course with less reliance on the dog's decision making – and therefore less chance to go wrong. However, there are times when you cannot physically get there in time to make the turn, or the line is such that a rear cross is the better option. For this reason, I am ready to use both moves when running courses.

The journey of learning to handle your dog in agility is making these discoveries for yourself. Enjoy!

Connie Sellers in
action at Crufts.

Rosie Cavill says...

I have working Cocker Spaniels, and although they compete with the best, they are not so easy to motivate as some of the the other breeds, such as Border Collies and Working Sheepdogs.

With my spaniels I start off by keeping training sessions really short and making sure they can get things right first time. I find that repetition turns them off so if they are struggling, I make the task easier so I can reward more regularly. Lots of paydays and jackpots are important, whether that is food or toy. What is most important is that you are giving a reward that the dog loves.

Some days can be frustrating and on those days I try to do one positive thing before moving on and trying on another day. Don't try to force it if it really isn't happening...

That being said, the more challenging your dog is to train, the more rewarding it is when you get it right. By working through the problems you really get to know your dog, and your partnership blossoms.

Trainer's Tip

IT'S COMPETITION TIME

You do not have to be super ambitious to enjoy agility but going to a show is an enjoyable day out with your dog and your agility friends. Anything you achieve in the ring should be considered a bonus.

Taking part in competitions is not for everyone. It's not a problem if you prefer to focus on training – maybe taking part in an informal club event – you are still spending quality time with your dog, keeping him physically fit and mentally stimulated.

If you do want to compete, you will have to wait until your dog is 18 months of age and you need to be confident that he will focus on you and be under control when he is off-lead. Bear in mind, the atmosphere at an agility show is incredibly exciting and your dog may well become hyped up and may struggle to concentrate. Your best bet is to take him to a couple of shows before you even think of competing. Spend the time walking around the rings, offering treats or a toy so that he is focusing on you, despite the distractions that surround him.

IS MY DOG READY?

If you are planning to compete, your dog will need to be registered with the relevant organisation and will need to be measured so he can run in the appropriate size category. Classes are divided between jumping and agility, and so if your dog is still being trained on the contact equipment (A-frame, dog-walk, seesaw), you could, initially, limit yourself to jumping classes. Weaves are included in most jumping classes so your dog will need to be doing a full set of 12 weaves before you enter.

ON THE DAY

On the day of the show you will need:

Accustom your dog to a show environment before you start competing.

- Ring card: Generally sent by post or available on-line, this will tell you the classes you have entered and your running order, which gives you your individual running order for each class. You are expected to run roughly in order.
- Ring plan: Sent with the ring card, this will give you a layout of the show, and you will see what is scheduled in all the rings.
- Fresh drinking water and bowl.
- Collar and lead: If your dog is competing, he can wear a collar, but there must be no attachments, such as a disc.
- Treat/toy: You cannot take these into the ring – though some organisations allow a toy if you enter as NFC (not for competition) – but you will need a toy or treats to help your dog to focus when you are waiting for your turn and, of course, to reward him when he has completed his round.
- Food and drink for you...
- Waterproof gear
- ....Dog!

Shows are time consuming and, with travelling time, you will probably be away from home for most of the day. You therefore need to decide what to do about feeding your dog. He has a taxing day so he needs food, but you must be careful that you leave at least two hours either side of running him and feeding him. A lot of handlers opt for giving a small meal before leaving home, and then giving a bigger meal on their return. You must also make sure your dog has plenty of opportunities to toilet – you don't want to be the red-faced handler who has to exit a ring when their dog is taken short...

WALKING A COURSE

The judge will set a course – either jumping or agility – which will be appropriate for your grade.

Before the class, you will have approximately 15 minutes to walk the course so you can find out where you are going and decide what you should be doing.
To make the most of course walking, adopt the following plan:

- Follow the numbers round the course so you know which way you are going.
- Now walk it again, working out the handling points and deciding your best options.
- Now walk it from your dog's point of view, seeing what he sees. This may alter your plan of action.
- Think of the verbal cues you are going to use, and when you are going to use them.
- Walk the course, putting in your handling points and verbal cues.
- If it is not too crowded, try running the course, which will give you a more realistic feeling of what it will be like when you do it for real.
- Try not to be influenced by your fellow course-walkers and stick to your own plan, regardless of what others are doing or saying. Every competitor has their own style of handling depending on their physical capabilities, the dog's speed, and his particular strengths and weaknesses. So make decisions based on what is best for you and your dog – and stick to your guns!

You want to be foot perfect when you get to the start-line, so how can you make sure you remember the course? Everybody has their own way of learning, and you need to find out what helps you to commit a course to memory. You may need to write it down, copying the layout and inserting your handling points. For others, it is more effective to walk away from the course, and then run through it envisaging each obstacle and memorising verbal cues and handling points. Bear in mind that it may be a couple of hours between walking a course and competing, depending on your running order, so some form of mental dress rehearsal should be considered essential.

YOUR ROUND

When you get to your ring, you need to book in with a member of the ring party, giving the number listed on your ring card. You will then have to queue alongside the ring, waiting until it is your turn to run. If you are lucky your dog will settle beside you but if you have an excitable type, you will need to keep him occupied, getting his attention with treats or a toy.

Just before your turn, you will be asked for your running order again so that the scrime (who is taking directions from the judge) can fill in your score card. Generally, the scrime (not the judge) will tell you when to start, but do not feel under pressure to go until you are ready and you have set your dog up in his start position. The timing starts as the dog clears the first obstacle.

As you negotiate the course, the judge will be marking the following:
- Dropped pole on a jump: 5 faults
- Refusal – running past the obstacle: 5 faults
- Missed weave entry or coming out of the weaves: 5 faults
- Missing a contact on the A-frame, dog-walk, seesaw: 5 faults
- Exceeding the time limit set for the course: faults will be deducted in line with your finishing time.

Rules and regulations may vary between governing bodies in terms of faults allocated and what constitutes an elimination. This may include
- Taking any obstacle out of order
- Three refusals
- Dog running out of the ring
- Dog toileting in the ring

So you can see there are plenty of chances to go wrong – but there is no better feeling in the world than when you get it right!

Always remember that agility is all about having fun with with your dog, regardless of your own personal ambitions. Your dog does not have to work for you; he chooses to do so because you are are offering the best and most rewarding of options. You are creating a partnership built on mutual trust and respect and – win or lose – agility training will enhance your relationship with your dog.

That is the greatest reward of all.

FURTHER INFORMATION

> **I**f by now you have caught the agility bug, you can carry on learning through a wide variety of books and dvds.

In the UK and Europe check out www.performancedog.co.uk for the best selection of books and dvds, plus a host of toys and other training aids.

In the USA, www.cleanrun.com and www.dogwise.com are the websites to use.

Many of the top handlers featured in this book have produced their own titles that can take you further in the sport.

Here is a selection, which you will find for sale on the websites listed above.

DENISE FENZI

- Dog Sport Skills, Book One: Developing Engagement and Relationship
- Dog Sport Skills, Book Two: Motivation
- Dog Sport Skills, Book Three: Play

SILVIA TRKMAN

- Agility Diary DVD

- Puppy Diary DVD

- Fun, Fast and Fabulous Weaves DVD

- Agility is Just a Game DVD

- Ready Steady Go DVD

- Running Contacts That Make You Smile DVD

- Cik and Cap DVD

- Tricks for Balance, Strength and Co-ordination DVD

- Tricks for a Great Bond DVD

- Tricks for Better Thinking Skills DVD

- Heeling is Just Another Trick DVD

DAVE MUNNINGS

- Q-Me DVD

- Turn Me DVD

GREG DERRETT

- Great Dog, Shame About the Handler DVD
- Great Dog, Great Handler DVD
- On Course to Excel DVD
- Agility Foundation Training DVD

SUSAN GARRETT

- Crate Games DVD
- Success with one Jump DVD
- 2x2 Weaves DVD
- Shaping Success
- Ruff Love

LEE GIBSON

- Agility Skills Development

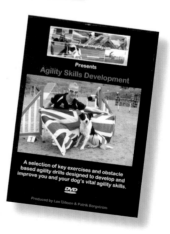